Economic Policy

Economic Policy

AN AGENDA
FOR THE
NINETIES

David Schwartzman

PRAEGER

New York
Westport, Connecticut
London

Library of Congress Cataloging-in-Publication Data

Schwartzman, David.
    Economic policy : an agenda for the nineties / David Schwartzman.
    p. cm.
    ISBN 0-275-93289-3 (alk. paper)
    1. United States—Economic policy—1981– . 2. Budget deficits—
United States. 3. Interest rates—United States. I. Title.
HC106.8.S39   1989
338.973—dc19   88-13779

Library of Congress Catalog Card Number: 88-13779
ISBN: 0-275-93289-3

First published in 1989

Praeger Publishers, One Madison Avenue, New York, NY 10010
A division of Greenwood Press, Inc.

Printed in the United States of America

∞™

The paper used in this book complies with the
Permanent Paper Standard issued by the National
Information Standards Organization (Z39.48–1984).

10 9 8 7 6 5 4 3 2 1

For Sol and Dot

CONTENTS

TABLES

ACKNOWLEDGMENTS

Persefoni Tsaliki provided research assistance, and Beverly Elliot and Karin Ray were helpful secretaries. Robert Ducas and Robert Heilbroner read an earlier draft, and I benefited from their advice. To all of these, thanks.

1

ECONOMIC PRIORITIES

THE DEFICIT AND THE DEBT BURDEN

Peter Peterson[1] and Felix Rohatyn[2] have been leading the chorus that the deficit is the number one economic problem. All the disasters go back to this source: the stock market crash, the rise (and fall) of the dollar, the huge trade deficit, and the decline of manufacturing. The deficit reached 6.3 percent of the GNP in 1983 and still was as high as 5.2 percent in 1986. Congress became panicky enough to limit its discretion in spending by passing the Gramm-Rudman-Hollings amendment. Even now that the deficit is down to 3.1 percent of the GNP, we still hear that it is the great problem.

Yet one should be skeptical about so simple a message. The deficit alone is unlikely to be at the root of such an assortment of economic events. This book shows that the rise of the dollar was not primarily due to the deficit. At the outset of the eighties, the Fed, confronted by a high rate of inflation, conducted a harsh, tight monetary policy. Paul Volcker, the chairman at the time, was prepared for the consequence of a rise in unemployment. The theory underlying the policy predicted that inflation could be brought down only at the cost of some unemployment. The theory did not predict that the dollar would rise, and Volcker did not expect this consequence. The other major development that was not anticipated was the growth in the demand for credit by business and consumers. This growth far exceeded the growth in the demand for credit resulting from the federal deficits. The economists who worry about the deficit ignore the Fed's monetary policy and the growth of private debt. Moreover, the rise in the dollar did not have a devastating effect on manufacturing. A careful look reveals that manufacturing has performed well. Some workers have lost their jobs, but this was due more to productivity growth than to the trade deficit. In general, economists have been too quick to see economic collapse and to blame the deficit for the loss of employment in manufacturing. Some economists have worried about the huge debt burden we are imposing on future generations. Reagan tripled the federal debt, and the interest on the debt now takes as much as 14 percent of total federal expenditures. Our children and grandchildren will bear a heavier weight.

But the burden may not weigh as heavily as we fear. If the Treasury is borrowing to finance buildings, roads, hospitals, and other investments, then why worry? In that case the gap between revenues and expenditures is no deficit. It is an investment financed by borrowing. No one accuses GM of running a deficit when it borrows to finance a new plant.

However, the federal deficit may exceed the investment spending. Whether or not it does, the answer depends on how we evaluate individual expenditures. Should we list the purchase of an aircraft carrier as an investment? Its life expectancy, unless a war comes, may be 20 years. It should be written off over that period, not over the period of construction. If we treat all weapons procurement in the same manner, then nearly half the deficit would vanish. The counterarguments are that today's new weapons are obsolete tomorrow and that a war will destroy them. Caution dictates the treatment of all defense expenditures as current expenses.

A more convincing case for long-term depreciation can be made for government buildings, roads, canals, bridges, and so on. Businesses would not write off such investments immediately. However, the case is not compelling. Government investments may be unproductive, while a private developer will not undertake a new building before it is certain of its marketability. Mistakes are made, but the developer bears the losses, not the general public. A partial allowance should be made for government investments, but it may not be enough to offset the deficit. Despite government investments, we may be piling up an excessive burden for future generations by running large deficits each year.

THE DEFICIT, THE INTEREST RATE, AND THE DOLLAR

In any case, our children's welfare is not our immediate concern. We read all the time that the deficit is wrecking the economy. If we believe Peterson and Rohatyn, it has ruined U.S. manufacturing. The links in the chain of argument are as follows. The deficit forces the Treasury to borrow heavily. This huge demand for loans raises the interest rate on bonds generally. Attracted by the high interest rate, Japanese, German, and British investors buy U.S. securities. To do so, they must buy dollars and sell yen, deutsche marks, and pounds, pushing up the exchange rates for the dollar. By selling yen to buy dollars, they raise the price of the dollar in yen—the exchange rate for the dollar in yen. A high dollar means high prices for U.S. goods in yen and other currencies. Expensive American machine tools do not sell well, and our exports fall. When the dollar is high the prices of Japanese and other nations' televisions, radios, machinery, and so on are low in dollars. One dollar can buy a lot more yen. Goods that you need yen to buy become cheap. Imports become cheap, and U.S. manufacturers lose sales at home. So Reagan's deficit has cost American workers their jobs.

There are some problems with this analysis. The dollar went up before Reagan's big deficits, so they cannot be the cause. Peterson and Rohatyn ignore the Fed's part in pushing up the dollar. They have forgotten that to slow down the consumer price index in 1980 and 1981, which was galloping at the annual rate of 13 percent, the Fed raised the interest rate to a high level. The Fed tightened money, the interest rate went up, and with it the dollar. Then came the recession of 1981 and 1982. The first big deficit came only in 1982.

Nor are the Fed and the deficit together the whole story. The eighties have seen the great American borrowing binge. Urged on by banks' advertising, consumers have had a love affair with their credit cards, and businesses also have been borrowing heavily. Lots of people and businesses have been running big deficits, not just the federal government. The interest rate rose because the private demand for credit went to new high levels.

What is more, the dollar has come down. In 1985 and 1986 the dollar fell while the deficit remained high. This apparently does not bother the deficit bewailers; now they blame the deficit for the drop in the dollar.

The deficit has caused no great economic disaster. True, the great rise in the interest rate in 1980 and 1981 cost many workers their jobs. People who might have built homes could not afford to make the interest payments. Business investment fell. The dollar rose and U.S. manufacturing lost sales both abroad and at home. But the deficit was not the source. This does not mean that the new administration can cavalierly dismiss the deficit as of no consequence, but it is not the great source of all our current economic problems. The Fed was behind much of the rise in the interest rate. The new Bush administration should understand that the Fed has exerted a great deal of economic power; it is a very activist, powerful organization. It brought on the recession of 1981–82 with its tight monetary policy. Before congratulating the Fed for its courage in fighting inflation, we should recall that it was attempting to correct the effects of its errors in 1976 and 1977 when its easy monetary policy exacerbated the already high rate of increase in prices. Fed Board Chairman Paul Volcker, who took office late in 1979, became a hero because he conquered inflation. But the heroism was made necessary because his predecessors fed the inflation.

In addition, it is not clear that Volcker's forecasts were better than those of his predecessors. It is unlikely that he foresaw the severe consequences of his actions. If he had known that the recession was to be be as bad as it was, he might have eased up. Nor is it likely that he expected the policy to drive up the dollar as much as it did. Since it is so poor at forecasting, the Fed should refrain from exercising as much power as it has in the past. If the Fed cannot correctly anticipate the consequences of its actions, then if it acts at all it should do so with great restraint. The administration cannot control what the Fed does, but it does have some influence. The Bush administration should urge the Fed to lean toward greater moderation.

THE DEFICIT AND THE STOCK MARKET CRASH

A major goal of the Bush administration will be to prevent a recession. We have enjoyed a long prosperity. It is seven years since the bottom of the last recession, and this is a long time as cycles go. The stock market crash of October 1987 threatened to bring one on, and the administration should try to avoid another one. If the stock market goes through another 500-point fall, it may bring the economy down with it. We have to understand the source of the 1987 collapse to develop a policy. Again we hear about the deficit. Peterson predicted the crash in the October 1987 issue of *Atlantic Monthly*. This success gave great weight to his diagnosis. However, the deficit was not the cause. The market had barreled along despite big deficits for five years. What is more, the deficit in 1987 was much smaller than it had been.

The crash was due to the Fed's action. Here we see another instance of the Fed exercising its great power and of its inability to forecast the results of its actions. The Fed raised the interest rate between February and September 1987. Inflation fears and pressure from foreign central bankers, who did not want to go on supporting the dollar in foreign exchange markets, led the Fed to push up the interest rate. The stock market was at a high level—the boom had been going on for a long time—and stock market prices generally are sensitive to movements in the interest rate. Hence the collapse.

The Fed acted to tighten the supply of money without full awareness of the effects of its policy. The immediate goal of preventing a further decline in the dollar blinded it to other consequences. The Fed did not anticipate the effect of its policy on the stock market. The Fed's vigorous intervention in the money market raised long-term as well as short-term interest rates substantially. After the fact it was no surprise that the Fed's actions produced the stock market disaster. Many people lost their savings, and many others lost their jobs. The important point to bear in mind is that the Fed did not expect to set off the stock market crash.

The Fed's economists neither are smarter than those elsewhere, nor do they have a clearer crystal ball. Economists predict interest rates, foreign exchange rates, GNP, employment, and so on on the basis of past observations. Unfortunately, past relationships did not continue. The past is not a reliable guide to the future, especially after people go through extremes of either inflation or recession.

The prospect of another stock market crash should not drive the Bush administration to drastically cut the deficit at whatever cost. The administration may not be able to do much, since it is the Fed that runs this country's monetary policy. Again, the administration should press the Fed to act in a moderate manner. The Fed thought prudence demanded vigorous action to prevent inflation, but it could not foresee the market collapse and a high risk of recession.

THE DECLINE OF MANUFACTURING

Peterson and Rohatyn join many economists in deploring the decline of U.S. manufacturing. We read that employment in manufacturing has dropped, and that many unskilled former assembly workers cannot find jobs. Those that do must work at low-paid jobs as baggers and stock clerks in supermarkets, as dishwashers and busboys in restaurants, and as orderlies and cleaners in hospitals. America can no longer compete. Peterson and Rohatyn point to the deficit and the high dollar.

Others, including economists Lester Thurow[3] and Robert Reich,[4] point to the low productivity growth of U.S. factories and the poor quality of the goods they produce. They do not see the deficit as the primary source of the decline; they agree that there has been a decline. For Thurow and Reich, Japan is the model. Its government has directed economic growth by subsidizing certain favored industries and by protecting them against import competition. The secret of Japan's success is the government's industrial policy. Thurow and Reich urge the United States to imitate the winner.

The AFL-CIO and the Cuomo Commission on Trade and Competitiveness also urge an industrial policy. The AFL-CIO specifies a long list of industries that should be protected against imports. The Cuomo Commission urges market-sharing agreements with other countries for industries afflicted by destructive competition arising from world overcapacity.[5] The commission believes that the fundamental problem is the world overcapacity in many industries. Both the AFL-CIO and the Cuomo Commission urge the government to set up a development bank to finance investment in unspecified industries, especially in depressed areas. The industrial policy for each industry will be run by a labor-management-government committee.

An industrial policy means government sponsored cartel agreements for some industries, protection against imports, and subsidies to firms in some industries. Taxpayers and consumers will pay the bills to maintain employment in some declining industries. Prices will be fixed at high levels, and where necessary the government will foot the bills.

The Bush administration should not undertake so radical a policy unless the economy—and more particularly manufacturing—is performing badly. However, we cannot say that manufacturing is performing badly simply because its employment has dropped without knowing the cause of the drop. According to industrial policy proponents, U.S. manufacturers have lost markets to Japanese and other competitors. Productivity growth has been poor, efficiency is low, costs are high and quality is poor. The condemnation of U.S. manufacturing performance is based on comparisons between Japan and the United States in a selected sample of industries, as well as on the drop in employment.

However, a full review of the evidence shows that the loss of jobs in manufacturing has been due largely to the growth of productivity, not loss of markets. Manufacturing has performed so well that it has produced more goods with fewer workers. Employment in this sector has fallen both absolutely and as a share of the total labor force. Machine operatives have lost their jobs and have had to depend on unemployment benefits as long as those last. Then they have had to become hamburger flippers. It is only when measured by employment numbers that manufacturing has declined. When measured by output, manufacturing has grown and has increased in importance. Manufacturing output has grown faster than the output of the service industries.

Even by international standards, the United States has not done badly. Manufacturing productivity growth has lagged behind that of Japan, but it has done well compared to other developed countries. Moreover, the lag behind Japan has many causes. It is doubtful that imitating Japan's industrial policy will remove the lag. We also hear that the United States has lost world market share in many products. This is inevitable when such less industrialized countries as South Korea and Taiwan are growing more rapidly than any developed country. Compared to other developed countries as a whole, our manufacturing industries have not lost market share. Japan is the only one whose world market share is growing more rapidly. Again, this has many causes. Perhaps now that the dollar is down from its earlier high level, U.S. manufacturers' market share will grow more rapidly than that of Japan's manufacturers.

American manufacturing has performed very well in the eighties. Manufacturers have become more efficient and productivity has grown rapidly. There is no need for an industrial policy. It is unfortunate that employment has declined and former workers have lost their jobs or have had to take low-paid jobs. However, to have made the productivity improvements while maintaining the same level of employment would have required an unrealistically great expansion of output. No industrial policy could have achieved such expansion.

THE BUDGET

The past Congress exaggerated the deficit problem. But a correct assessment of the problem should not prevent the Bush administration from raising taxes and reducing expenditures. Unless a recession intervenes, reducing the deficit does not present an insuperable problem. Moreover, there will be demands for additional expenditures. The quality of services provided by state and local governments has deteriorated to unacceptable levels, and these governments are in a poor position to raise the necessary funds. There will be other demands for new expenditures.

The deficit rose because Reagan, together with Congress, reduced tax rates while raising defense expenditures. Reagan said no deficit would arise because with lower tax rates businesses would reap more of the benefits of their investment and workers would retain more of their earnings. Everyone would work harder, incomes would go up, the lower tax rates would generate more taxes, and the budget would be in balance. This was the supply-side theory. The theory overestimated the incentive effect of the tax reduction, and the budget went into deficit.

The personal income tax can be raised easily by the three or four percentage points needed to eliminate the deficit. If there is too much resistance to raising personal income tax rates, then the administration might propose imposing a value-added tax, which many countries in Europe already have. The value-added tax is similar to a sales tax, but it is imposed at each stage of production and distribution on the value added to the goods or services at that stage. It is a great revenue producer. A tax rate of 2 or 3 percent would take care of the deficit. No great economic problems would result from raising the funds either from higher personal income tax rates or from a value-added tax.

On the expenditure side, the big items are defense, social security, medicare, interest, and others. Interest and social security are sacrosanct. The cost of medicare is more likely to rise than to fall with the growing demand for medical care by the elderly. Congress has recently agreed to meet the costs of catastrophic illnesses for the elderly. The "other" category has already seen sharp cuts, particularly expenditures for poverty assistance. This category is unlikely to offer significant opportunities for reducing the deficit.

Defense offers the greatest opportunity. However, without fundamental policy changes, we are unlikely to see great reductions in these expenditures. The major categories of expenditures are personnel, operations and maintenance (O&M), and procurement. The administration cannot cut either personnel or O&M substantially as long as it maintains its present commitments to Western Europe. The withdrawal of U.S. forces would permit very great reductions in expenditures, but only if the forces are reduced overall, not merely restationed in the United States.

Such a drastic change would require a reassessment of the Soviet threat and of the ability of the Western Europeans to maintain adequate defenses. We may be ready for such a reassessment. Since World War II the United States and its allies have exaggerated the Soviet threat. In recent years the estimates of Soviet defense expenditures have come down substantially. We also now know that apparently aggressive actions by the Soviet Union in the Berlin and Cuban crises were not motivated by expansionist goals. Moreover, Western Europe now is rich enough to provide an adequate defense on its own. The forces need not be so large as to guarantee victory over invading Soviet armies. The Soviets will be deterred by the prospect of a costly war.

Procurement can be cut substantially without signficantly reducing U.S. defense capabilities. The navy's maritime strategy, which previous administrations have endorsed, calls for an enormously expensive 15-carrier fleet. In the event of the planned-for West European war, the carriers and their escort vessels will undertake to attack the main Soviet submarine base at Murmansk in an effort to assure the safe passage of troops and supplies by sea from the United States. The strategy has many detractors among military experts. The merit of the expensive B–1 bomber program also is dubious. There are other opportunities for cutting defense expenditures.

Defense expenditures have been justified in the past on the basis of their percentage of the GNP and some arbitrary rate of growth. In earlier periods defense expenditures consumed a larger fraction of the GNP than they did under Carter. Therefore, not enough was being spent. Moreover, the Soviets' rate of growth of defense expenditures exceeded our own, and they spent more of their GNP on defense than we did. The estimates of the Soviet rate of growth have been exaggerated, and the USSR has spent more of its GNP on defense than we have because it has a much smaller GNP. Nor are the historical comparisons a good guide. Our GNP is much larger now than in Eisenhower's day, we are not fighting a war in Korea or in Vietnam, and the appraisal of the threat has changed. In any case, the approach to estimating what we need for defense on the basis of percentages of the GNP does not encourage a serious assessment of particular expenditures. The army acquires certain very dubious weapons, such as the Bradley armored troop carrier, because the money is there. The greater the funds that are appropriated, the more items are purchased that are further down on the priority list.

However, the opportunities for reducing defense expenditures without a major policy change are limited, and a major change, if one comes, will be gradual. It will not come quickly enough to eliminate the deficit in the next two to three years.

Overall, there will be new demands for more spending. State and local services are in a bad state. Recently many people, including conservatives like William Bennett, Secretary of Education in the Reagan cabinet, have become alarmed over the state of education. Crime rates have gone up enormously since World War II. Daily we see the homeless sleeping in subway stations. Expenditures for the chronically ill will probably grow. More money is needed to maintain the existing roads and bridges.

The general conclusion is that to balance the budget, the Bush administration will have to raise personal income tax rates or impose a new tax.

2
THE BURDEN OF THE
PUBLIC DEBT

Nearly everyone writing about the subject attacks the current federal budget deficit because it raises the rate of interest and foreign exchange rates for the dollar. Here we look at another important and much more obvious aspect of the deficit problem: the climbing public debt and the burden it creates for our children and grandchildren. If they care for history's verdict, the Bush administration and Congress will try not to load them with a huge burden.

Our grandchildren may have to pay higher taxes, because the deficits add to the public debt. Worse, the resulting high interest payments may create an explosive growth of the public debt by forcing future administrations to borrow to make these payments. The United States could become another Brazil. Our generation may be remembered as profligate, careless, and selfish. However, a big debt need not impose a huge burden. The government invests in highways, education, and other productive facilities and activities that will enhance future incomes. Future generations will not complain about paying interest on a debt that financed their bridges. We first present the case of no government investment. Assuming no productive investment by the government, must the new president and Congress raise taxes or cut expenditures to keep future taxes from climbing to unconscionable levels?

ASSUMING NO PRODUCTIVE INVESTMENT

As of late 1988, the current federal deficit was about $150 billion, or 3.1 percent of the GNP In 1986 the deficit was much higher in relation to the GNP—5.2 percent.[1] Congress cut expenditures to bring the deficit down. Nevertheless, the deficit retains its political prominence. The one thing that the candidates in the primaries and during the election campaign were unanimous about was that the deficits could not continue at their current levels. But, except for one candidate, they dared suggest neither an increase in tax rates nor the specific expenditures that should be cut. That candidate was Governor Bruce Babbitt, and he did not last long.

The future debt burden—say in 25 years—will not be heavy if the GNP grows so rapidly that taxpayers have much higher incomes or if administrations quickly increase taxes or cut expenditures. Some assumptions have to be made about economic growth and future deficits to estimate the burden that we shall pass on. When we say the debt burden, we mean interest payments on the public debt as a percentage of the GNP. The higher this percentage is, the larger will be the proportion of our incomes that we will have to pay in taxes merely to pay the interest on the public debt.

The estimate of the burden depends heavily on these assumptions. A reasonable assumption is that the administration and Congress will do nothing. Past administrations have found it easy to put off raising taxes, and future administrations may be no more courageous, especially if recessions cut taxpayers' incomes. Cutting expenditures will also be difficult. Imagine also that economic growth is at the average annual rate of 2.6 percent—the average annual rate of growth of real GNP between 1980 and 1987. The annual growth rates over this period ranged from −2.5 percent between 1981 and 1982—the worst recession year, to 6.8 percent between 1983 and 1984—the year of rapid recovery. The period includes both recession and rapid recovery years, so the growth estimate is not biased by excessive representation of either. Other years saw growth rates of 1.9, 3.0, and 2.9 percent.[2] It is reasonable to assume that growth will continue at about 2.6 percent per year on the average, and that recessions will be mild and of short duration. In other words, our luck holds out and nothing shockingly bad happens.

We also assume that the current real interest rate remains the same. The real interest rate on the public debt is approximately 4.6 percent. The nominal rate—the one that the government says it is paying—on average is about 9.1 percent. But inflation keeps bond-holders from receiving this much. They lose whatever the inflation rate is times their investment. The current inflation rate (April 1989) is about 4.5 percent. So the real rate is 9.1 minus 4.5 percent. This is how we arrive at our estimate of the real rate. Since the demand for credit has been rising and the real interest rate along with it, to assume a constant real rate probably leads to an underestimation of the future debt burden.

Now let us stretch our imaginations. We suppose that the growth rate, assumed to be 2.6 percent per year, holds out for 25 years. Tax receipts are maintained at 19.3 percent of the GNP and federal expenditures at 22.4 percent. The deficit remains at 3.1 percent of the GNP. This assumption also biases the estimate of the future debt burden downward. Federal expenditures for medical care, highways, and education also will grow. As we will see, there is little room outside defense for expenditure reductions. Defense ex-penditures may not decline, even as a percentage of the GNP. We have to make some assumptions because any serious problem aris-ing from the deficit will be felt only years from now and only if future administrations continue to run large deficits. The selected assumptions tend to understate the future burden.

Under these conditions, the burden of the debt will grow in relation to the GNP. Realistically, we assume that the debt keeps on growing—none of it is ever repaid. The burden will grow be-cause the deficit as a percentage of the GNP is higher than the rate of growth of the GNP. Taxpayers' incomes grow at the same rate as the GNP, but interest payments grow faster. Ignoring for the moment the growth in the interest burden that is due to the growth in interest payments, we look only at the rise in interest payments that is due to a constant deficit resulting from expenditures on defense and other functions of government, as a share of the GNP. By the year 2014 interest payments on the federal debt will make up as much as 6 percent of the GNP, compared to the 1988 figure of 3 percent.

But this is not all. Suppose the federal government gives in to Wall Street and balances the budget from now on except for interest payments, which continue to be financed by borrowing. The interest burden will continue to grow simply because the interest rate—and here again I mean the real interest rate—is higher than the economic growth rate.

The total interest burden in 2014 will be the sum of the interest payments due to the continuing deficit plus the interest payments on loans taken to pay the interest. The total comes to 9 percent of the GNP. Obviously, this will be impossible, since we have assumed that total federal expenditures then will make up the same percentage of the GNP as in 1988—22.4 percent. Forty percent of the budget will be spent on interest payments.

ASSUMING GOVERNMENT INVESTMENTS

But the government does make productive investments. We do not insist that businesses pay for their investments out of current receipts because we expect the buildings and equipment purchased to be productive over a long period. The investments will be recouped and a return will be earned from either the resulting increase in sales or a reduction in costs. Why should we demand that government investments be paid out of current tax receipts? Robert Eisner has argued that since much of the increase in the public debt is used to finance investments, it does not create a burden for later generations.[3] The interest payments they make will be balanced by the resulting growth in income. No one expects consumers to pay cash for the houses they buy or businesses to pay for machinery out of current receipts.

Estimates of investment by the federal government indicate that they are about as large as the deficit. As Eisner points out, the Office of Management and Budget (OMB) included in investment outlays in fiscal 1984 $34 billion for construction, $67 billion for equipment, $7 billion for inventories, $41 billion for research and development, and $22 billion for education and training. These expenditures do not include those defense expenditures that might be classified as investments, such as aircraft carriers, submarines, aircraft, airfields, and housing. The civilian investment expenditures alone summed to $171 billion. These expenditures were nearly the same as the deficit for that year. For fiscal years 1985 and 1986 the estimates of federal investment are $195 billion and $215 billion, respectively, which are close to the corresponding deficits.[4]

If the investments are as large as the deficits and the return from the investments in additional services equals the resulting interest payments, then we need not worry. Future generations will bear no additional burden. The rise in the GNP resulting from better roads, a more efficient postal service, and so on will compensate for the rise in interest payments.

But the improvements in public services are unlikely to warrant the additional interest payments. Unlike business investments, public investments need not meet market tests. We have heard of boondoggles. Some expensive water conservation projects probably would not be undertaken if the farmers who benefited from them had to pay their costs. Every month former Senator William Proxmire used to present the Golden Fleece Award to a publicly funded research project. Nevertheless, some public investments are productive. The burden of the public debt in 2014 will not be as great as the estimate has suggested. Americans will enjoy some benefits from the expenditures.

CONCLUSION

The uncertainty about the productivity of public investment expenditures argues for balancing the budget. If we could be sure that such expenditures produced as high a return as private investment, we would not have to be so cautious about deficits. It is easy for Congress and the administration to spend and borrow. When the administration and Congress no longer are constrained by the limits of current tax revenues, the demands of particular interest groups are hard to resist.

If the burden of the debt in 2014 is anywhere nearly as high as the estimates indicate, we have much to be concerned about. Unless taxes are raised before that happens or expenditures are reduced, we will probably go through another inflationary spiral to cut the debt. Inflation is the traditional method of reducing the debt. Those who minimize the deficit problem point out that in 1946 the federal debt exceeded the GNP. Today it is less than half as much. What these optimists forget is that since 1946 the price level has risen nearly six times. The inflation eliminated much of the debt. Bondholders simply were not repaid. If we do not stop adding to the debt at the present high rate, we can expect a repetition of the inflation of the seventies.

3
THE DEFICIT AND
THE INTEREST RATE

President Bush must decide pretty quickly whether or not to proceed to eliminate the allegedly grave economic infection afflicting the United States. However, the infection may not be nearly as serious as the exhorters say. This chapter concerns only the effects of the deficit on the interest rate. The interest rate is critical, for it is through the interest rate that the deficit presumably raised the value of the dollar and threw thousands of steel, textile, and auto workers out of their jobs in the early eighties. The president should know that the diagnosticians of the failure of U.S. manufacturing have misread the data. They are wrong about the importance of the deficit for the rise in the interest rate, and as Chapter 6 shows, they are wrong about the failure of manufacturing. Manufacturing has not declined. This chapter shows that the rise of the interest rate in the early eighties was not due largely or primarily to the deficit.

OTHER FACTORS IN THE RISE OF THE INTEREST RATE

Intent on raising a scare, Peterson omits the other, more important contributors. He is silent about the Federal Reserve System's anti-inflation, tight monetary policy. As far as Peterson is concerned, the Fed has nothing to do with the interest rate. Yet, led by Paul Volcker, the Fed stoutly fought inflation, not weakening when auto workers lost their jobs and farmers went bankrupt. The tight monetary policy reduced the amount of funds available for loans while the demand for loans kept rising. Because the demand grew relative to the supply of funds, the interest rate, which is the price borrowers have to pay for funds, rose.

Nor can Peterson, as a banker, plead ignorance of two developments that have caused more damage than the deficit: the rise in the demand for credit and the fall in velocity. The interest rate was driven up by the huge growth in the demand for loans. These have been times of temptation. Households, corporations, and state and local governments have been on a borrowing binge. Consumers increased their reliance on credit cards, and businesses and state and local governments have accumulated debts. The unprecedented high deficits notwithstanding, the Reagan administration was not the great offender that many have said. The financial press misleads by pointing only to the federal government, which succumbed less to temptation.

"Velocity" is a technical term referring to the turnover rate of money. Money includes currency and balances in checkable accounts at banks, savings and loan associations (the thrifts), brokerage houses, and other financial institutions. If John spends $30,000 per year and keeps an average bank balance of $3,000, the velocity of his bank balance is 10. The balance turns over 10 times. If he increases his average balance to $6,000, then the velocity falls to five. If John's average bank balance increases, he is spending less, or he may have sold some stocks and bonds and put the proceeds in his bank account. Rather than earning a higher return, he may prefer not to worry every time he writes a check that he does not have a large enough bank balance to cover it. He does get interest on his bank balance, and the difference between the bank rate and the rate available from short-term securities may not be worth the inconvenience of having only a little cash on hand.

The average velocity for the economy as a whole is calculated by dividing the GNP by a measure of the amount of money. The measures going from the narrowest to the broadest definition are M1, M2, and M3. Economists now appear to prefer M2, which includes currency, demand deposits, and savings deposits.

For reasons that no one is certain about, velocity, regardless of how it is measured, has fallen in the eighties. People are keeping larger balances in their checkable accounts. Neither higher incomes nor greater expenditures explains this change. One reason may be that since the late seventies depositors have been able to earn interest on balances in their checkable accounts. They do not have to invest in securities to earn a return. In any case, the fall in velocity is another source of the rise in the interest rate.

A drop in velocity is as much a rise in the demand for money as is growth in the demand for loans. People borrow and are willing to pay interest to make certain purchases for which they may not have cash readily available. They pay interest to have the cash. Larger bank balances also represent a demand for cash, even though depositors do not explicitly pay interest. They pay interest implicitly by giving up the higher interest rates available from less liquid investments.

We should not omit the changes that have reduced the rate of interest. Peterson fails to mention that the erosion of national barriers to financial transactions has attenuated the deficit's effect on the interest rate. More and more in the age of instant communications the U.S. Treasury borrows in a world money market. The world's bankers are constantly in communication with each other buying and selling currencies. When London bankers buy dollars, they usually are doing so for a person or a corporation somewhere in the world who wants to invest in U.S. securities. A small rise in the U.S. interest rate relative to interest rates in other countries will bring in a flood of orders from investors everywhere, not only American investors. Seeking the highest return, British Petroleum's treasurer must decide daily how to invest the multinational's idle funds, as must the treasurers of Hoechst, Imperial Chemicals, and of other multinationals. Handling millions of dollars, marks, and yen, they will shift money among investments in various countries when they can make even small gains in interest rates. In this market the U.S. Treasury's borrowings have little effect on market rates. If the U.S. market were insulated from the rest of the world, the Treasury would be borrowing a large share of the total funds available. A large deficit, which would force the Treasury to sell a large issue of bills or bonds, would depress the prices of U.S. securities generally. But in an open world market the Treasury's influence is much smaller. When Peterson says that the deficit has raised the rate of interest substantially, he exaggerates the Treasury's influence in the world market.

It may be unfair to pick on Peterson, whose views many economists share. Despite its popularity, the argument that the deficit is a dangerous disease is flimsy. The economists who have raised the alarm know very little. Their forecasts of the effects of fiscal and monetary policy on the interest rate have been poor. The interest rate is difficult to predict. Economists do much better when they evaluate the effects of an oil import tax or of other measures affecting individual industries than in gauging the effects of macroeconomic policies. It is not only the international nature of the money market that presents problems. I have mentioned the growth in the demand for credit and the decline in velocity, neither of which are well understood. Changes in the demand for credit and in velocity are difficult to predict.

A major problem is that bankers, money managers, and corporate treasurers are not predictable automatons responding to the Fed's twists of the monetary dials. On the contrary, the money managers at Bankers' Trust, Salomon Brothers, Exxon, and the Chemical Bank try to predict the Fed's actions. Everyone in the market is predicting everyone else's behavior including that of the Fed and the Treasury. It is hard to tell the regulators from the regulatees. Investment managers do not simply respond as expected to changes in the Fed's manipulation of the supply of money.

Keynes taught economists to regard the economy as a hydraulic machine with fluids coursing through tubes marked GNP, employment, money, consumption, and investment. The Fed could manipulate the flows by working the money valve, which directly and through the interest rate controlled investment and consumption, and therefore GNP and employment. Providing the Fed and the administration cooperated, the economy could be kept going at full employment without inflation. Unfortunately, the money managers make the system break down by anticipating what the Fed will do.

Since what the Fed fundamentally is trying to control is not economic magnitudes but the actions of people who have their own expectations, its policy may be ineffective. Professional investors handle most of the money in the market. Pension and mutual funds are run by professional investors, who have the same data as the policymakers and employ the same theories in analyzing trends. These money managers forecast unemployment, inflation, GNP growth rates, the trade balance, capacity utilization rates, and many other economic indexes. Not only do they attempt to forecast movements in interest rates and prices resulting from the actions of market participants, but they also try to anticipate actions by the Fed, the administration, and Congress. The Fed may try to raise employment by increasing the supply of money and thus spending. But the banks may anticipate inflation and raise the rate of interest to compensate, frustrating the policy. Not only the bankers and people in the money markets form expectations, union leaders, business people, and workers generally also get to believe that prices will continue rising after many months of inflation, and they make their plans accordingly. The Teamsters, along with other unions, win wage increases calculated to compensate for an assumed rate of inflation. Department-store buyers pay higher prices than they have earlier, expecting that the sale prices in the next season will cover the costs plus a margin. The buyers anticipate a certain rate of inflation. Builders pay high wages and high prices for materials, expecting rentals and sale prices to be high. These expectations are difficult to dislodge, and in the absence of very severe restrictive actions by the Fed, the inflation will continue to spiral. Thus, given the expectations of inflation, unemployment could accompany high inflation in the seventies.

Expectations of inflation have rendered the Phillips curve, which is the basis of public policy, obsolete. It continues to be the basis because we have nothing to replace it; an obsolete theory is better than none. The Phillips curve envisions a tradeoff between the inflation rate and the unemployment rate. Phillips observed that in Britain over a long period unemployment went down when prices rose; when prices fell unemployment rose.[1] This relationship was also observed in more recent years in the United States. But in the seventies the Phillips curve broke down. We now had both high inflation and high unemployment.

Monetary and fiscal policies are grounded on the monetarist and Keynesian theories, which do not take expectations into account. Although in either theory high unemployment is incompatible with high inflation, during the seventies the economy suffered from both. Caught between the opposing goals of raising employment and bringing prices down, the floundering Fed alternated between stimulative and restrictive policies. The restrictive policies induced recessions without restraining inflation greatly, and the stimulative policies fueled the inflation without raising employment to an acceptable level. However, the failure of the theories did not discourage activism by the Fed. Indeed, Chairman Arthur F. Burns believed that his seat-of-the-pants judgments were more reliable than any theory.

The Fed's policymakers have not been inhibited by uncertainty about the consequences of their decisions. They have played recklessly with the money supply with devastating consequences. As a result, the economy has been on a roller coaster. During the high inflation period bondholders and savers generally suffered greatly. The severe recession cost many their jobs. The Fed did not expect easy money to bring on wild inflation, and they did not expect the tight monetary policy that followed to depress the economy as much as it did. As Chapter 4 shows, the Fed did not expect its policy to drive up the dollar and so destroy exporters and businesses competing with imports. Nor was the tight monetary policy of 1979 through 1981 the end of the Fed's reckless activism. In 1987, as we see in Chapter 5, the Fed raised the rate of interest, bringing about the stock market crash. The record argues that since the Fed cannot foresee the effects of its policies it should not have as much power as it does.

THE DEFICIT AND THE INTEREST RATE

Countless worthy causes demand funds. A deficit, of course, allows Congress to indulge more causes than an unwilling public will pay for. Before Keynes it was the modern equivalent of printing currency. But a self-imposed discipline declared deficits anathema until Keynes prescribed them as good medicine for depressed economies. Theories rule the world, and new theories displace old ones. Inspired by the new Keynesian doctrine, in 1946 Congress passed the Employment Act, promising full employment. The administration, assisted by the newly-created Council of Economic Advisers (CEA), was to pursue appropriate policies. When the new doctors of the economy expected a rise in unemployment, they would advise the administration and Congress to increase spending without raising taxes, or they would call for a reduction in taxes. Deficits were no longer anathema. They were to be an instrument. The old balance-the-budget rule was rejected as part of the superstitious heritage.

The new therapeutic science called for the economic diagnosticians to predict the GNP, employment, the interest rate, and the rate of inflation. When they expected a rise in unemployment, they were to order more spending but not higher taxes, or they were to order reductions in taxes. Inflation or expected inflation called for the opposite remedy.

Economists also designed a role for the Fed. When unemployment threatened to get worse, the Fed was to stimulate demand by opening up the money spigots and when a high rate of inflation threatened, the Fed was to tighten them down. The Fed puts money into people's hands by buying the Treasury's bonds or 90-day bills. The theory is that the sellers will spend some of their newly acquired cash. This immediate effect is leveraged by its effect on bank reserves and on bank lending. The Fed pays money into the bank accounts of the sellers. The new money is also added to the commercial banks' reserves deposited with the Fed. Because their reserves have grown, the banks can increase their loans. The borrowers of the new loans now will spend more than they otherwise would have. Inflation calls for the Fed to contract consumer and business spending by selling securities. When the Fed sells securities, the sellers have less cash. Their banks lose reserves when they pay the Fed, and they have to cut the number of loans they make.

The other stimulative effect of Fed purchases is through the rate of interest. When the Fed buys Treasury securities, it bids up the prices of securities generally. A rise in bond prices is the same thing as a fall in interest rates. John pays $1,000 for a promise of an annual interest payment of $90—the rate is 9 percent. Purchases by the Fed raise the price of such a promise to $1,025. If John were to buy the same security now, he would pay $1,025. The rate of interest has fallen to 8.78 percent. Fed sales of securities have the opposite effects. They reduce security prices, thereby raising the rate of interest.

Despite the passage of the Employment Act and his appointment of the ardent Keynesian Leon Keyserling as CEA chairman, Truman retained the old dread of deficits. Congress was even more loyal to the old faith. Eisenhower too was a fiscal conservative, as was his CEA Chairman Burns. I have already mentioned Burns in connection with his later position as Fed chairman under Nixon and Ford. Deficits did come but they were the unintended consequences of the Korean War and of the recession beginning in 1958.

When Kennedy came into office the Keynesians finally got their chance. Kennedy himself was a reluctant disciple, but he appointed Keynesian Walter Heller to the CEA chairmanship. Nineteen sixty was not a good year. Unemployment stood at 5.5 percent, higher than through most of the fifties. One of Kennedy's campaign themes was that it was time to get the economy going again. He was all for economic growth. Unemployment was even higher when he actually took over. In 1961 it was as high as 6.7 percent. The inflation rate was less than 1 percent. Obviously unemployment was the top agenda item. Heller convinced Kennedy to press for a public works program consisting of some big highway and building construction and slum clearance projects, and he also persuaded him to support a tax cut. After 1960 only the year 1969 did not see a federal deficit. The balance-the-budget leash had been broken.

As late as the eighties, Walter Heller and other Keynesian economists continued to take credit for the maintenance of full employment during the sixties. They were the ones who persuaded Kennedy to cut taxes, and the Fed's easy money policy was consistent with this goal. What was more, Keynesian policies prevented recessions in the seventies and eighties from reaching the depths of the Great Depression. This view of the validity of the Keynesian prescriptions prevailed through much of the seventies even among conservative economists. But by the eighties skepticism was rampant.

Economists now took the opposite position. The deficit caused workers to lose their jobs. If the deficit had this effect, it did so by raising the rate of interest. The interest rate is at the center of the puzzle. We will see how the deficit may raise the rate of interest in a moment. We first have to understand how a high rate of interest affects employment. The unemployed lost their jobs because the high rate of interest in the United States raised the exchange rates for the dollar, making U.S. goods expensive and foreign goods cheap. The U.S. interest rate is linked to the dollar: A high interest rate means a high dollar. The high interest rate in the early eighties attracted foreign investors. For that matter, U.S.-based multinationals also shifted their investments from foreign to U.S. securities. They could get a better return from U.S. investments than from Japanese, West German, or British securities. But to shift their investments the multinationals had to buy dollars in the foreign exchange markets. They had to sell their German, Japanese, and British securities. The investors received marks, yen, or pounds, which they had to sell in the foreign exchange markets to obtain dollars. These transactions raised the exchange rates for the dollar. As the demand for dollars grew, the investors had to pay more in yen, marks, and so on, for a given number of dollars. The rise in the dollar meant that the prices in yen, marks, and pounds that the Japanese, Germans, and British had to pay for American cars, textiles, and machine tools increased. More important, the prices Americans had to pay in dollars for imports of Japanese, German, and other foreign goods fell. U.S. importers had to pay for the foreign goods in foreign currencies, but they had to pay fewer U.S. dollars for a given amount of the foreign currency. When the American consumer bought a Honda, he or she would be paying a lower price in dollars, even though in yen the price had remained the same.

The deficit-induced high interest rate may also have thrown people out of work by taking the profits out of investments. GM borrows to finance the building of a new plant. It will not go ahead with building the plant if the interest payments are so high as to leave small profits.

Deficits were viewed as stimulative through the sixties and seventies, perhaps because in most years the deficit was small. But even the large deficit in 1968, when it reached 3 percent of the GNP, was regarded as stimulative. Indeed, to this day economists blame this deficit for the ensuing inflation. President Johnson would not take the political risk of raising taxes to pay for the Vietnam War plus the Great Society. The deficit added to total spending and to the pressure on prices. At the time no one argued that it depressed business activity by raising the rate of interest.

Of course, the Treasury was not alone in the market. Although unemployment was at a low level and there was no need for a stimulative policy in 1967 and 1968, the Fed added inflationary fuel, pursuing a recklessly liberal monetary policy. In 1968 the inflation rate rose to over 4 percent and the unemployment rate was only 3.6 percent. The stock of money grew at a rate that whipped up inflation. The following year the Fed applied the brakes. The Fed's job is to stabilize the economy, not to speed it up and then bring it to an abrupt stop. However, at this point it brought on a recession. Worse, the recession failed to stop inflation. Except for 1971 and 1972, the inflation rate remained high through the seventies. Looking back, Keynesian economists blamed Johnson for inflation combined with unemployment. Once inflation was let loose, it was hard to rein in. People expected inflation to continue. The Fed could only cool the inflation by forcing people to revise their expectations, and this demanded a severe recession, much more severe than those that the Fed induced in 1970 and 1974. Johnson may deserve much of the blame. But after economists jettisoned the no-deficit rule, no politician could survive with a high-tax platform. It is not even clear that the 1968 deficit was to blame for the later high inflation. The Fed's liberal monetary policy in some of the years contributed to it.

When the deficit reached the new high of 5 percent of the GNP under Reagan, economists turned the other way. Now the view was that the deficit depressed business. The world has not changed that much since the sixties. Why should the federal deficit have different effects in the eighties than in the sixties? We have to investigate the relation between the deficit and the interest rate. Of course, the new view was greatly influenced by the size of the deficit.

When the Treasury pays out more than it receives in taxes it does not order the Mint to print more currency. Instead, the Treasury borrows by selling short-term promissory notes—Treasury bills, which come due in three months or six months, or it sells bonds, which may not come due for as long as 30 years. These bills and bonds make up the public debt. New ones are issued as those outstanding mature and have to be repaid.

The Peterson argument is that the deficit has raised the rate of interest because it has forced the Treasury to raise vast sums. The Treasury is the largest borrower by far in the United States; in 1982 it raised as much as 40 percent of all the credit issued (Table 3.1).

The borrowings, according to the argument, have driven up the interest rate.

As Table 3.1 shows, the rate of interest did rise. We have to distinguish between the real and the nominal rate of interest. The nominal rate of interest is the one paid in dollars that are not adjusted for price increases. Thus, currently the federal funds rate, which is the rate paid by banks on their overnight borrowings from other banks, is 9.71 percent. But inflation cuts the real return. Since the inflation rate is 4.5 percent approximately, the real rate is 9.7 minus 4.5 percent, or 5.2 percent.

It is the real rate that concerns us. Table 3.1 shows that the real rate was negative in 1975, 1976, and 1977, when the rate of inflation was higher than the nominal rate of interest. Strangely, instead of borrowers paying lenders, lenders were paying borrowers. Genius though he may be at making deals, Donald Trump happened to choose the right period to make his deals. He probably did not plan on inflation. When he was developing some of his biggest deals he did not have to pay for the money he used; he made money simply by borrowing and using the money.

From a negative level the interest rate rose sharply each year, reaching a peak of 6.7 percent in 1981. Over the period 1976 to 1981 the nominal rate of interest rose: The real rate went up for this reason. The rate of inflation did not fall. Only in the following year did inflation decline.

Now, if the deficit is the culprit, then the real rate should rise with the percentage of the total borrowings made by Treasury. If its share did not rise, then the demand for credit by other borrowers was growing more rapidly, forcing the interest rate up. Table 3.1 shows the Treasury's share of total borrowings and the real interest rate. We can see that the Treasury's share reached a peak in 1982. However, the real rate reached its peak the year before. Moreover, the rise in the interest rate between 1976 and 1981 was associated with fluctuations in the Treasury's share, not with a steady upward trend. Between 1982 and 1984 the Treasury's share fell sharply, while the interest rate fell the first year and rose the second year.

Economics is never so simple that we can pin a change in interest rates, the price level, the wage level, or other macroeconomic variables on a single cause. Clearly, other influences than the deficit have been at work. Not only have households and businesses in-

Table 3.1

Treasury Borrowings as a Percentage of Total Credit Issued in the United States and the Real Federal Funds Rate, 1975-1987

	Treasury/ Credit (%)	Federal Funds (%)		Treasury/ Credit (%)	Federal Funds (%)
1975	42.0	-3.98	1982	40.2	5.86
1976	26.3	-1.35	1983	32.9	5.19
1977	17.3	-1.16	1984	26.1	6.43
1978	13.9	0.63	1985	26.1	4.80
1979	9.7	2.30	1986	25.5	4.11
1980	21.6	4.36	1987	21.1	3.01
1981	22.0	6.68			

Sources: Treasury borrowings and total credit from *Economic Report of the President 1985*, p. 308; ibid., 1988, p. 332; and *Federal Reserve Bulletin*, August 1988, p. A42. Federal Funds rate from *Economic Report of the President 1988*, p. 330.

Note: Real federal funds rate calculated as nominal rate minus GNP implicit deflator.

creased their borrowings more than the Treasury has, but the Fed has been active. The high rate of interest is due more to the Fed and to the growth of loans to the private sector than to the deficit.

THE FED AND THE INTEREST RATE

In the late seventies the Fed had to take action to stop prices from going up any faster. In 1979 the consumer price index (CPI) was climbing at the unbelievable rate of 13 percent. The Fed already had begun to cut the amount of money people had available to spend. It applied more pressure. However, it could not bring the rate of inflation down without inducing what turned out to be a severe recession. It was never a question of stopping inflation completely. Even to slow down the pace of the rise in prices needed a recession. To understand why this was so, we need to look at the theory underlying the policy.

The total value of goods produced (GNP) equals the quantity of money (M) times velocity (V), which, as we have seen, is the number of times money turns over in a year. When we multiply M by V, we obtain the total spending in a year, which is the same thing as the GNP. Now, the GNP valued in current prices differs from the real GNP. The GNP equals the volume of goods and services produced, real GNP (RGNP), times the average price level (P). Thus,

$$\text{GNP} = \text{RGNP} \times P = M \times V.$$

To fight inflation, the Fed reduced M, the quantity of money. The theory was that reducing M would have the effect of reducing P. For all of the effect to fall on P, V had to remain the same. People had to keep spending money as fast as they did before. If they speeded up the rate at which they spent money, a reduction in M would have no effect on P. If they slowed V down, then the reduction in M would bring P down even faster than the Fed intended. Further, for the reduction in M to have the intended effect on P, RGNP would have to remain the same. People would have to keep buying goods at the same rate, and factories would have to keep turning goods out at the same rate.

However, when the Fed cut the money supply, it reduced RGNP,

Table 3.2
Percentage Changes in M2 from
Previous Year, 1968–1987

	(%)		(%)
1968	8.0	1978	8.0
1969	4.1	1979	8.0
1970	6.6	1980	8.9
1971	13.5	1981	9.9
1972	13.0	1982	8.8
1973	6.9	1983	11.8
1974	5.5	1984	8.4
1975	12.6	1985	8.5
1976	13.7	1986	9.0
1977	10.6	1987	3.3

Source: Economic Report of the President 1988, p. 325.

Note: M2 includes currency, bank deposits, and other checkable accounts.

or output, as well as inflation. The Fed never intends to cut output—more output is always desired. But the Fed cannot cut the rate of inflation without also reducing output and therefore employment. The problem is very serious when unemployment is high, as it was in 1981.

Table 3.2 shows an extremely active Fed. The Fed has sometimes raced the economy and generally has favored high employment over low inflation. Between 1968 and 1987 the growth of M2 in a year varied between 3.3 percent and 13.7 percent. The annual growth of total output varied much less: between a decline of 2.5 percent and a growth of 6.8 percent. In the early seventies the Fed tried to bring the economy out of the recession. Adding fuel to the inflation, M2 grew faster than current-dollar GNP. Inflation reached 5.7 percent in 1971 when the economy was emerging from the recession and unemployment was falling. That year the Fed was pumping money into the economy at such a high rate that M2 rose by 13.5 percent. The Fed again accelerated the inflation between 1975 and 1977. M2 rose at the rate of 12.6 percent in 1975, while inflation raged at 9.8 percent. The primary goal was to lift the economy out of the simultaneous recession; output fell by 1.3 percent that year and 8.5 percent of the labor force was unemployed.

Other years the Fed applied the brakes. Thus in 1969 M2 grew by only 4.1 percent. The increase was sharply lower than in the previous year, when it was 8 percent. In 1973 the growth of M2 came down to 6.9 percent, a sharp drop from the 13 percent increase in 1972. In both years it was trying to bring down the inflation rate. But the result was a recession in 1970 and another beginning in 1974. Indeed, the Fed's actions had more effect on total output than on the inflation rate.[2] In 1978 the Fed began to tighten again. Nineteen eighty was a repetition of 1979—a recession combined with a raging inflation. It was a severe recession. The economy did not begin to recover before 1982. The Fed's restrictive policy was effective only by first inducing a recession. Contracting the money supply did not slow down inflation directly or immediately but only after a recession had set in. In 1983 money was loosened again.

The Fed continues to maintain a tight money policy out of fear of inflation. In 1987 the rate of inflation accelerated modestly. But the Fed evidently regarded even the small rise as a signal of worse to come. The other factor influencing the Fed was the desire to prevent the dollar from falling further in foreign exchange markets. (We deal with this in Chapter 5.) Because of these concerns, the Fed reduced the growth of the money supply from the 9 percent rate of 1986 to 3 percent. During the months March to August 1987 the interest rate rose. In August when the present chairman, Alan Greenspan, took over from Volcker, the Fed raised the interest rate that it charges banks for loans by half of a percentage point. The Fed took this action only one month before the stock market crash. Stockholders feared that the Fed was intent on raising the interest rate. We cannot ascribe the stock market crash entirely to the Fed's policy, since stock prices had risen for an extended period. Stock prices were high and yields therefore were much below what an investor could earn by buying bonds. Nevertheless, the Fed was throwing its weight around, and the market reacted.

The analysis is complicated by the increases in the rate of velocity. The Fed can hardly forecast GNP if velocity is changing. A 1 percent rise in velocity is equivalent to a 1 percent rise in M2, which is also the case on the negative side. The effect of a decline in velocity may be even more devastating than the effect of the Fed's actions.

If the Fed decides that the inflation rate is too high and cuts the money supply, the economy may sink into a worse recession than the Fed believes necessary. Instead of accelerating steadily at a modest rate, the velocity has jumped around and, much to everyone's surprise, velocity has decelerated since 1982.

Between 1978 and 1980 the Fed tightened money. It allowed the stock of money to grow at a rate of between 8 and 9 percent. This policy is judged to be tight because the rate of growth was considerably less than the rate of growth of current-dollar GNP, which was boosted by a high rate of inflation. Remember that GNP = RGNP × P. If money goes up at the same rate as current-dollar GNP, it presumably will have no effect on either RGNP or P. In 1979 M2 increased by 8 percent, while current-dollar GNP went up by 11.5 percent. Thus, the Fed was being restrictive. It was not allowing current-dollar GNP to continue growing at the same rate. If velocity had continued to accelerate at a constant steady rate, the Fed's tightening would have had little effect. The effect of this clamping down was enhanced by the concurrent slowdown in V. Thus the rate of growth of V went from 5 percent in 1978 to 0 percent in 1980. Moreover, in succeeding years the velocity has been declining by as much as 5.1 percent.

Indeed, if velocity increases had been maintained, the Fed would have had to take more extreme measures to stop inflation. Usually Paul Volcker, the Fed's chairman beginning late in 1979, is credited for the stern anti-inflation policy, which presumably was what did the job. But the fall in velocity had a greater effect than did the Fed's policy.

Why has velocity declined? One explanation is that banks now pay interest on their demand deposits. People have less incentive to shift idle balances into short-term securities than they did earlier. The difference between the rate of 5.5 percent, which is what the banks pay, and the 5.7 percent return paid by the Treasury in 1987 on three-month bills was not enough to warrant shifting. Permitting the banks to pay interest on their demand deposits may have had the unexpected effect of slowing down velocity.

The deficit has been a minor element in the rise of the interest rate. Much more important were the fall in velocity and the tight monetary policy between 1979 and 1981—before the onset of Reagan's large deficits.

CONCLUSION

The deficit should not be dismissed, but it was not the main source of the rise in the interest rate. The rise preceded the large budget deficits, and we have seen that during the eighties the amount of credit extended to households and businesses grew more than the loans to the Treasury. The rise in the rate of interest was due more to the growth of demand for credit by the private sector than to the federal deficits.

Moreover, it is not obvious that the federal deficit has a lesser claim than private borrowing. Some of the deficit finances additions to the productive capacity of the nation. Some of it is for buildings and roads, which in a business would be treated as capital expenditures. Paying for education by issuing bonds also is proper. Future generations should pay for the resulting enhancement of productivity. Chapter 2, the Burden of the Public Debt, takes up this topic.

The Fed also had a hand in raising the interest rate. By restricting the growth of the money supply to slow down inflation, the Fed raised the rate of interest. Moreover, the Fed continues to restrain the growth of the money supply out of a continuing fear of inflation.

We have seen that people are keeping more cash in checkable accounts now, which raises the interest rate further. The velocity of circulation has come down. Uncertainty regarding velocity has complicated the Fed's task. The effect of a small reduction in the supply of money may be enhanced by a drop in velocity. A large part of the rise in the interest rate in the eighties was due to the decline in velocity. It contributed more than the deficit and perhaps more than Fed policy.

We should also be aware of the fact that the United States is now part of the world market. The flows of money across borders deprive the Fed of a good deal of its power. If the rate of interest is high, it may be simply because the world interest rate is high. The real interest rate was not uniform across countries before 1980, and interest rates did not always move together. Evidently the U.S. market was somewhat insulated, and the Fed had considerable power over the interest rate. But since 1980 world interest rates have converged, and they move together. The Fed has lost much of its old power. It still exercises an independent influence. Money does not move as freely between the United States and other countries as it does within the United States. An easy money policy may still stimulate the economy and indeed bring on inflation. But the Fed will have greater difficulty promoting full employment. The interest rate may remain high and even rise because foreign central banks refuse to follow suit. The Fed will also have greater difficulty suppressing inflation. Interest rates may remain low despite a restrictive monetary policy.

Finally, the discussion takes it for granted that the interest rate is high. This judgment is based on historical experience. Between 1980 and 1986 the real interest rate exceeded the levels reached in the previous 40 years. Since then it has come down closer to the historical average. But the historical comparison is not decisive. Even the interest rate at its peak in 1981, when the real federal funds rate reached 6.7 percent, was not high. We cannot call the interest rate high when the private demand for credit continues to grow. Businesses found it profitable to invest increasing amounts of funds, and consumers did not allow the high interest rate to inhibit their borrowing.

Nor was there any slowdown in business investment after the recession ended in 1984. Over the period of 1980 to 1987 the economy experienced a rapid growth in the stock of machinery, buildings, and capital generally. The growth was not confined to the service sector, contrary to a popular assertion. The stock of capital in manufacturing grew even more rapidly than in the service sector. Apparently the interest rate was not high enough to stop companies from building new capacity.

At the time of this writing, the interest rate is not excessive. The historically high interest rate does not signify an excessively high interest rate. President Bush should not decide to cut the deficit because of its effect on the interest rate.

4

THE INTEREST RATE
AND FOREIGN
EXCHANGE RATES

Peterson blames the budget deficit for the trade deficit. If we believe Peterson, the budget deficit raised the interest rate and therefore exchange rates for the dollar between 1980 and 1985. This popular analysis holds that Reagan and Congress gave up markets and therefore jobs for Americans by stubbornly refusing to raise taxes: The budget deficit is central.

But, as the preceding chapter argues, the deficit has been less important in the rise of the interest rate than were the Fed's tight monetary policy and the changes in the credit and money markets. Moreover, the dollar may not be as closely tied to the interest rate as Peterson says. Although the interest rate has remained high, since 1985 the dollar has fallen. The puzzle becomes more complicated when we see that despite the fall of the dollar since 1985, the trade deficit remains high.

We read other explanations of the trade deficit. Congressman Richard Gephardt blames Japan's and South Korea's import restrictions. Not all the restrictions are obvious violations of the General Agreement on Tariffs and Trade (GATT). Some appear to be safety standards. Gephardt proposes retaliatory measures against countries with persistently large trade surpluses with the United States.

Robert Reich blames the trade deficit on the decline of American competitiveness. Reich says that the Japanese achieve greater productivity than Americans do, and their cars, television sets, and so on have won a better reputation for quality than this country's products. According to Reich, hard work alone is not responsible. The Japanese manufacturers benefit from government planning and support. If the Bush administration wants American manufacturers to compete effectively, it will have to give them similar assistance.[1]

Writing about the growth of Japanese productivity, Lester Thurow stresses the bonus system of compensating workers' participation in decision making. U.S. manufacturers must become more competitive; they must imitate Japanese methods. Moreover, the U.S. government should encourage the growth of promising, high-tech industries. Government agencies should actively promote particular industries.[2]

These arguments ignore the dollar. If the trade deficit were due to Japanese import restrictions or to inferior American productivity, then the trade deficit would have pushed the dollar down. Instead, between 1980 and 1985 the dollar rose. So neither import restrictions nor competitiveness explain the trade deficit. The exchange rates for the dollar are the key to the trade deficit. The sharp rise of the dollar made U.S. manufactures more expensive than those of other countries.

President Bush must understand the sources of the rise and fall of the dollar to make appropriate decisions about the budget deficit, trade policy, and industrial policy.

The president should also know that the Fed's actions have had devastating effects on imports and exports. The rise of the dollar, which did so much damage to the U.S. economy, was partly due to the Fed's tight monetary policy between 1979 and 1981. The Fed did not expect its policy to have this effect. The Fed should have been aware of its poor forecasting ability and should have restrained both its stimulative actions in the mid-seventies and its restrictive actions later. The president should encourage self-restraint by the Fed.

THE RISE AND FALL OF THE DOLLAR

American Honda dealers sell dollars to buy yen to pay for imports. Currently ¥100 fetches $.7583, or $1 is equivalent to ¥131.88 When the dealers import more cars, they raise the demand for and therefore the price of yen expressed in dollars. Viewed the other way, they increase the supply of dollars and therefore depress their price in yen. Conversely, when Japan Airlines sells yen to buy dollars to import more Boeing aircraft, it increases the demand for and therefore the price of dollars in yen. Increases in U.S. imports raise exchange rates for foreign currencies while they lower the exchange rates for the dollar. A boom in exports does the opposite.

The analysis of exchange rates would be simple if exporters and importers were the only ones who bought and sold currencies. Indeed, the theory of exchange rates assumes that this is so. It is when we introduce capital transfers that the trouble starts. But let us go along with the assumption that the foreign exchange departments of the great commercial banks in New York, London, Tokyo, Frankfurt, Singapore, and in other cities serve only exporters and importers, and that members of neither group speculate in currencies. If, at the current exchange rates, woolen cloth and other traded goods were more expensive in the United States than in Italy, the demand for Italian goods would grow, and the lira would rise relative to the dollar. Exchange rates that did not accord with domestic prices of traded goods could not persist.

Under these conditions the real exchange rates would change by small amounts. The nominal exchange rates might go through swings because countries experience different rates of inflation. The hyperinflation in Mexico brought down the peso's exchange rate for the dollar. But the real exchange rates—the nominal exchange rates corrected for relative changes in prices—will not climb or fall sharply. The theory of exchange rates argues that they will reflect the purchasing power of the various currencies.

In recent years, however, exporters and importers have not dominated exchange rates. Speculators and investors have been the ones pushing exchange rates up and down. The speculators are hard to tell from investors, since both try to predict changes in exchange rates. The only difference is that the investors commit their funds for longer periods. The same company may engage in both activities. Some of the biggest currency traders are the multinationals, whose officers must decide where to invest their funds. If the Global Corporation buys U.S. government bonds, it will do so because the rate of return relative to the riskiness is higher than for other securities. The calculations include a forecast of the exchange rates for the dollar. When the dollar swings as much as it has in recent years, what might otherwise have been an investment becomes a largely speculative activity.

Speculation may accelerate movements in exchange rates initiated by the Fed's monetary policy. When the Fed raises the interest rate, it may push the dollar up. Speculators may push it even higher. Global's treasurer may judge that the Fed will maintain higher interest rates than are available in West Germany. Global will buy dollars to buy U.S. securities, converting its holdings of other currencies. Alternatively, it may simply purchase dollars, which need not be kept in the United States. Multinationals keep deposits denominated in dollars in banks in various countries. These are known as Eurodollar deposits. If Global's treasurer expects the dollar to rise because he expects the Fed to raise the rate of interest, he may buy dollars for deposit in Eurodollar accounts.

Data on U.S. international transactions show large inflows of foreign capital, but they need not signify a rise in the demand for U.S. securities, bank deposits, or plants and other physical assets. They may reflect an excess of U.S. imports over U.S. exports. The capital inflows include increases in foreign-owned U.S. bank deposits, securities, and so on, which correspond to the excess of imports over exports. The current account has been in deficit because we have been importing more than we have been exporting, What we owe foreigners becomes an inflow of capital. When the Import-America Corporation pays the Export-Japan Company for imports, they are included in the statistics on payments on current account. If total payments exceed total receipts, the United States shows an unfavorable balance on current account. In recent years U.S. imports have exceeded exports by far, creating an unfavorable balance on current account. Export-Japan may keep the receipts in a U.S. bank or it may convert the receipts into U.S. securities. In either case, it will accumulate U.S. assets—the transaction will result in a capital inflow. If Export-Japan does not want to keep U.S. assets, then it will sell its dollars. But someone else will hold them; they will not go out of existence.

Of course, capital inflows also include purchases of U.S. securities by foreigners and by multinationals that are not the result of U.S. imports. Global may decide to buy U.S. Treasury bonds as an investment or because it expects the dollar to rise.

As a result of such speculative or investment transactions, the

Table 4.1

Indexes of Multilateral Trade-weighted Nominal and Real Values of the Dollar (1980 = 100)

	Nominal	Real
1980	100	100
1981	118	119
1982	113	132
1983	143	138
1984	158	152
1985	164	156
1986	128	122
1987	111	107

Source: Based on *Economic Report of the President, 1988,* p. 371.

dollar's real exchange rates have gone through wide swings since 1980. Between 1980 and 1981 the index of the real value of the dollar in terms of other currencies increased 19 percent (Table 4.1). By 1985 this real value had increased by 56 percent. The next year it dropped by 34 percentage points, and in the following year by another 15 percentage points. By 1987 the dollar was almost back where it had been in 1980. We can also see that nearly all of the change in the nominal rate was accounted for by the real rate. The changes in the nominal rate thus were not due to changes in the purchasing power of the dollar relative to other currencies.

Of course, in 1985 imports were much cheaper than in 1980. Americans had to pay 36 percent less in dollars for an average bundle of imports whose prices in foreign currencies had not changed. In foreign currencies U.S. goods were much more expensive. On the average, foreigners had to pay 56 percent more for U.S. goods. The effect was the same as it would have been if other countries had raised their tariffs against imports from the United States by that amount. The United States would have made loud protests and imposed retaliatory tariffs. But it could hardly protest a rise in the dollar, particularly since it was largely the product of its own monetary policy.

Not surprisingly, exports fell and imports rose. The $32 billion trade surplus of 1980 became a trade deficit. In 1987 the trade deficit reached a peak of $120 billion. Although the trade deficit clearly was the result of the rise in the dollar over most of the period, as we have seen, the cry went up that American industry was losing its competitiveness.

U.S. competitiveness was not the problem. If it were, the change would not have been so sudden. Welders, lathe operators, engineers, and electricians did not forget their skills, nor did the Japanese suddenly become highly skilled. American goods became more expensive because the dollar did. And the dollar went up partly because foreigners wanted to invest in the United States. They could earn a higher rate of return from U.S. securities than from those of other countries. Speculation was another reason. Speculators expected the dollar to continue rising.

Because the wide swings of the dollar hurt many firms competing in world markets, people wonder whether the world should return to the gold standard and fixed exchange rates. The dollar's value in marks or in yen, it is hoped, would stay within a narrow range, as it did before 1971 when Nixon decided that the United States would no longer buy or sell gold at the fixed price of $35 per ounce—when the United States went off the gold standard. Before 1971 the United States bought and sold gold at that price; central banks in other countries bought and sold gold at prices quoted in their own currencies. The exchange rates of the currencies themselves were the outcome of these transactions. If the Treasury paid $35 for an ounce of gold, and the Bank of England's price was £12.50, then the value of the pound in terms of dollars was 35/12.50, or $2.80. The selling prices set by the Treasury and the various central banks were slightly higher than their purchase prices. Movements of the exchange rates thus were limited.

After Nixon decided that the United States would no longer buy or sell gold at a fixed price, the dollar was free to float in relation to other currencies. Henceforth, exchange rates would fluctuate in response to the demand for and the supply of the various currencies.

However, Nixon's decision was forced by the same kinds of pressures that have caused the dollar to fluctuate since then. It was not a voluntary decision based on an analysis of the effects of changes in the dollar. The problems arose from differences in the rates of inflation of various countries, which in turn reflected different monetary and fiscal policies. If the inflation rate was higher in Britain than in the countries with which it traded, then the pound declined even under a fixed-exchange rate system. The Bank of England might attempt to maintain the pound's value by buying pounds in foreign exchange markets. It might also raise interest rates in an effort to keep money at home. The government might impose quotas on imports. But as long as prices in the UK were rising faster than elsewhere, these attempts were futile. Thus, in 1967 the UK devalued its currency from $2.80 to $2.40.

Nixon's decision was devaluation under another name. In the late sixties inflation accelerated. West Germany's and Japan's exports to the United States grew, while U.S. exports did not grow, so these countries built up their dollar reserves. Foreigners could not tolerate this situation much longer. Thus, the shift to floating exchange rates was triggered by the UK's demand for $3 billion in gold. Instead of devaluing the dollar, which is to say raising the price of gold in dollars, the United States decided to stop buying or selling gold.

Currently, exchange rates move daily as those engaged in trade, investors, and speculators buy and sell various currencies. The central banks intervene from time to time when they believe that a currency has risen or fallen too far. We have what is called a dirty float. After the meeting at the Plaza Hotel in New York in September 1985 where the central bankers agreed that the dollar had risen too much, they intervened in the foreign exchange markets by selling dollars. The action succeeded in bringing the speculative boom to an end. The boom may have been about to end in any case, since the real interest rates in West Germany, Japan, and the United States had converged.

The central banks are not always so successful. After the Louvre Conference in February 1987, where they agreed that the dollar had fallen enough, they bought dollars. But the decline continued. Apparently, the forces bringing the dollar down were very powerful and the central banks were unwilling to buy up enough dollars to stop the decline. They were unwilling to risk increasing their dollar holdings indefinitely when a further decline in the dollar was possible. The larger their dollar accumulations were, the more they stood to lose from any decline in the dollar. At some point they would want to sell dollars.

The central banks do not rush to support currencies when they drop below certain announced levels or to prevent currencies from exceeding those levels—they do not maintain fixed exchange rates. However, from time to time they intervene when they believe that speculation rather than the underlying economic forces have driven exchange rates to unreasonable levels. The central banks may be wrong, and they may fail. But they do intervene.

The dollar exchange rates rose and fell between 1980 and 1987 because investors first wanted dollar-denominated securities and then wanted to exchange them for securities denominated in other currencies. Why did they shift? The data in Table 4.2 can be interpreted as follows.

In 1981 the Fed's tight monetary policy raised nominal and therefore real short-term interest rates. Prices still were rising, but the rate of inflation was only a little higher than in the preceding year. The rise in the nominal interest rate was gigantic, with the result that the real short-term interest rate went from −.15 percent to 5.98 percent. In the next two years the fall in the inflation rate kept the real interest rate high; only the nominal rate fell off. The long-term rates also rose sharply in 1981 and went to historically high new levels in the subsequent years.

Before 1981 prices were going up very rapidly in this country. One of the results was a negative rate of interest. The nominal rate of interest did not rise sufficiently to compensate for the high rate of inflation. Lenders continued to be willing to accept a low, even a negative rate of interest. The tight monetary policy resulted in a sharp rise in the nominal rate of interest and thus in the real rate. The rate of inflation remained high that year. It fell only the following year.

The real rate of interest in the United States may go up without the dollar following suit. For the dollar to rise, the real rate has to go up relative to the real rate in other countries. The West German and Japanese inflation rates were low throughout the late seventies and early eighties, and the nominal rates of interest did not move greatly. Throughout the period the nominal interest rates in these countries were below those paid in the United States. In 1980 the federal funds rate in the United States—the rate paid by banks for overnight loans—was 13.4 percent compared to money market rates in Japan of 10.9 percent and 9.1 in West Germany. The rate

Table 4.2
Real Short-Term and Long-Term Interest Rates in the United States, Japan, and West Germany and Differences, 1977–1986 (in percentages)

| | Short-Term | | | | | Long-Term | | | | |
| | Rates | | | Differences | | Rates | | | Differences | |
	United States	Japan	Germany	U.S.-Japan	U.S.-Germany	United States	Japan	Germany	U.S.-Japan	U.S.-Germany
1978	0.32	0.53	0.69	-0.21	-0.37	0.88	2.26	3.09	-1.38	-2.21
1979	-0.04	2.28	1.73	-2.32	-1.77	-1.91	4.11	3.23	-6.02	-5.14
1980	-0.15	2.94	3.73	-3.09	-3.87	-2.12	1.23	3.13	-3.35	-5.24
1981	5.98	2.53	5.80	3.45	0.18	3.32	3.76	4.90	-0.44	-1.58
1982	6.19	4.27	3.96	1.92	2.23	6.85	5.39	4.26	1.46	2.59
1983	5.84	4.63	2.14	1.22	3.70	8.09	5.66	4.64	2.44	3.45
1984	5.93	3.82	3.13	2.11	2.80	8.18	4.53	5.43	3.65	2.75
1985	4.61	4.41	1.35	0.20	3.26	7.48	4.29	3.05	3.19	4.43
1986	4.90	4.20	4.80	0.70	0.10	5.80	4.30	5.70	1.50	-0.10

Sources: Based on IMF, *International Financial Statistics Yearbook 1986*, pp. 347, 421, 689; *International Financial Statistics March 1987*, pp. 65, 66, 71.

Notes: Nominal short-term rates represented by federal funds rate in the United States and money market rates in Japan and Germany. Nominal long-term rates represented by long-term government bond yield in the United States, government bond yield in Japan, and public authority bond yield in Germany. Real interest rates estimated by subtracting change in consumer price index from preceding year from nominal rates.

of increase of the consumer price index in the United States was 13.5 percent, compared to 8.0 percent in Japan and 5.3 percent in West Germany. The real short-term rates of interest thus were in the United States −.1 percent, 2.9 in Japan, and 3.8 in West Germany. Real long-term rates also were lower in the United States than in the other two countries. Under these conditions there was little incentive for investors to move funds from West Germany and Japan to the United States. Therefore, the U.S. dollar did not rise.

The fall in the U.S. inflation rate did not come before 1982. Thus the rise in the real interest rate in 1981 was entirely due to the rise in the nominal interest rate, which in turn was the product, as Chapter 3 showed, of the decline in M2 and in velocity. The rise in nominal interest rates in the United States was large. It was sufficiently large for real short-term interest rates in the United States at that time to exceed those in Japan and West Germany. Real long-term rates in Japan and West Germany still were above those in the United States. U.S. long-term rates rose more slowly, possibly because investors doubted that a tight monetary policy would persist in the recession that had set in.

Accordingly, in 1981 it became profitable for investors to move funds out of Japan and West Germany into the United States. The higher profitability of investment in the United States continued until at least 1984. In the following year, short-term rates in Japan were approximately equal to those in the United States. Long-term rates in the United States continued to be well above those in Japan through 1986. In 1986 both short-term and long-term rates in Germany were approximately the same as in the United States.

Thus in 1986 real interest rates in the United States came into line with those in West Germany and Japan. The call for a halt to the rise in the dollar in September 1985 by the finance ministers and central bankers at the Plaza Hotel meeting was well timed.

The dollar fell throughout 1986 and 1987. Investors did not want to hold onto the dollar, despite the fact that real interest rates in the United States were approximately the same as in Japan and were higher than in West Germany. In September 1987 the real federal funds rate was about 3.2 percent (7.22 minus a 4 percent rise in the CPI), compared to a real money market rate of 3.4 percent in Japan (the inflation rate was zero), and a real money market rate of 2.7 percent in West Germany (3.8 nominal rate less 1 percent inflation rate). The dollar should not have fallen any more since September 1987. Investors should have been withdrawing funds from West Germany and investing them in U.S. or Japanese securities. The dollar dropped another 8 percent against the mark and 9 percent against the yen. More recently the dollar has risen and fallen again. It is difficult to anticipate small weekly movements in the dollar.

CONCLUSION

The rise of the real interest rate, which preceded the deficit, brought about the rise of the dollar in 1981. The higher real interest rate was due to a combination of the drop in velocity, the rise in the demand for credit in the United States, and the Fed's tighter monetary policy. Since 1985 the dollar has dropped. The fall was not due to the decline in the deficit, which reached its peak in 1986, but to the convergence of real interest rates in the United States, Japan, and West Germany. Speculators shifted into other currencies because there was no reason to expect the dollar to continue rising.

5

THE STOCK MARKET CRASH

One of the Bush administration's goals will be to prevent a recession. We face the possibility that another stock market crash will bring one on. The October 1987 crash may have been due to the budget deficit, as has been alleged. We have to understand how important the deficit was for that crash.

The long climb in stock prices was fed by a speculative mania that may have ended in a crash, whatever policy was followed by the Fed and the Treasury. The long march of the stock market from 1982 to 1987 tripled equity values. How much higher could they go? Dividends did not grow enough to warrant the climb. According to Standard and Poor's, the average dividend on common stock fell from 5.81 percent of the stock price to 2.69 percent.

But the optimists in the stock market do not have only themselves to blame. The Fed has to accept part of the responsibility, for between March and September 1987 the Fed had raised interest rates. The yields on stocks could not keep falling while bond yields rose. Indeed, there is no law that says that stock prices must fall if yields fall. If yields fall along with interest rates, there is no lower limit even at zero. In the period of high inflation in the late seventies real interest rates fell below zero.

The Fed tightened the money supply because the dollar was falling rapidly in foreign exchange markets, and foreign central banks were pressing it to stop the fall by raising interest rates. Another influence was the recurrent fear of inflation.

The Fed's action had two effects on the stock market. The direct and more powerful effect of the rise in the interest rate was to depress prices. However, the rise in the interest rate moderated the fall in the dollar, which if unchecked threatened to bring about a collapse in stock prices. The falling dollar weakened market support. The Japanese, West Germans, and other foreign owners of American stocks were keeping their funds tied up in dollars. They were concerned that further drops in the dollar would cancel any gains they might make in stock prices. Ultimately the Japanese cared only about the gains measured in yen, and similarly for other foreigners. On balance, however, it is clear that the Fed's policy helped bring about the crash.

In other words, the crash was not due to the deficit. The major policy decision leading to the market crash was that of the Fed. Neither the administration nor Congress was to blame.

The policy of raising the interest rate was not the Fed's alone. The Reagan administration had a hand in developing it. Treasury Secretary Baker too wanted to stop the dollar's decline. Probably neither the Fed nor the Treasury expected the rise in the interest rate to upset the market as much as it did. Except in the last month before the crash, the rise was slow, and no single small increase in the interest rate would have precipitated such a huge selloff. More- over, the policymakers' primary concerns did not include the effect of a rise in the interest rate on the stock market. The dollar was at the center of attention, inflation was the second worry, and the stock market came in as a poor third—if the Fed and Treasury fretted about it at all.

Again, as in the mid-seventies when the Fed pursued an easy monetary policy and the late seventies through 1981 when it tight- ened up, the Fed did not foresee the full consequences of its policy. Had it foreseen the crash, it would not have raised the interest rate as much as it did.

THE RISE IN THE INTEREST RATE

The average yield on long-term U.S. government bonds rose from 7.25 percent in March 1987 to 9.42 percent in September. This rise represented a drop of 23 percent in bond prices, which was as large as the drop in the Dow on Black Monday. Had it happened on a single day, the drop in bond prices would have caused great alarm. Over several months the drop failed to catch much attention. Nevertheless, financial analysts employed by pension funds, mutual funds, investment bankers, and brokerage houses were well aware of what was happening. The prices of stocks could not continue to rise much longer while bonds fell. Even after subtracting the inflation rate from the yields on bonds, they were higher than yields on stocks. Ordinarily, the nominal yield on stocks is not adjusted for inflation because, unlike interest payments on bonds, dividends presumably will rise with inflation. The more the prices of stocks rose, the lower did their dividend yields fall— dividends were not rising at nearly the same rate as the prices. When investment analysts saw bond yields going up and up, stock prices had to fall sooner or later. The last month before the crash the long-term government bond yield rose from 8.76 to 9.42 percent—a big jump after a steady rise. The only thing propelling the continuing advance in the stock market was the self-fueling expectations of further advances. The market was becoming increasingly fragile. A big selling spree could be ignited by some bit of bad news.

A critical question thus is: Why the rise in the interest rate? In the past the interest rate has risen because investors have expected inflation. In the months preceding the crash, inflation was a worry for many—at one point the annual rate of inflation was as high as 8.4 percent. The previous year the average rate had been 3 percent. It began to look as though the Fed had given in to inflation.

However, the Fed had not given in. Fighting hard to keep inflation down and the dollar from falling more, the Fed tightened the money supply causing interest rates to rise. The Fed was responsible for the rise in the interest rate, and thus at least partially responsible for the crash. We can see that the Fed tightened money by comparing the annual rate of growth of M2 in 1987 with the rate in 1986. In 1986 M2 had grown 9 percent. In April 1987 the rate of growth of M2 from the previous month expressed as an annual rate was 5.6 percent. In the next three months the rates were, respectively, .3, .6, and 2.5 percent. In August the growth went up to 6.5 percent, still far less than in 1986. In September the growth was at the annual rate of 5.7 percent.[1]

The Fed adhered to its restrictive policy right up to the time of the crash. The first thing that the new Fed chairman, Alan Green-span, did on his appointment was to raise the discount rate from 5.5, where it had been for over a year, to 5.95 percent. When member banks borrow from the Fed to add to their reserves they pay a rate of interest, which is called the discount rate.

WHY THE FED RAISED THE RATE OF INTEREST

As we have seen, the inflation rate was behaving erratically early in 1987. The Fed was afraid that its easy monetary policy in 1986 was precipitating inflation a year later. Fed actions had delayed effects. An injection of money into the economy lit a fuse that did not set off inflation for a year or more. The Fed tried to make up for what it feared had been undue liberality the previous year. But the picture was complicated, since the liberality had been accom-panied by a decline in velocity, as we saw earlier.

However, the Fed probably was worried more by the continuing fall of the dollar. To see why the dollar had become a problem, we have to understand that the Fed's tight monetary policy at the beginning of the decade had pushed the dollar up to a very high level. At that time Volcker was concerned only with inflation. Both Fed and Treasury officials knew that a restrictive policy might bring on high rates of interest, followed by a recession. Higher costs of financing investment would stop companies from buying new plants and machinery. The drop could snowball, precipitating a fall in consumer spending. These fears, of course, were warranted. The recession of 1981 to 1983 was severe.

What Volcker did not anticipate in 1980 was the rise in the dollar. The daily trading of billions of dollars for other currencies was new. The Fed decided to raise the interest rate without full aware-ness of the consequences for the dollar and for exports and imports. The Fed's actions raised not only the absolute interest rate but also the interest rate relative to interest rates abroad. It is the relative real interest rate that matters. Multinationals and individuals who are looking for profitable investments pay attention to relative real rates of interest. The Fed's policy raised the relative real rate of interest in two ways. It raised the nominal interest rate and it re-duced the rate of inflation, thus having a double impact on the real interest rate, which is equal to the nominal rate minus the inflation rate.

Corporate treasurers and foreign investors rushed to buy U.S. securities, which suddenly became attractive. To buy U.S. dollars they had to dispose of foreign currencies, bank deposits, and securities. The dollar rose. Between 1980 and 1985 the trade-weighted average exchange rate for the dollar rose 56 percent, after correcting for price changes in the various countries. In other words, the real average exchange rate for the dollar rose that amount. In computing the average, weights are assigned to the various countries' currencies based on the volume of their trade with the United States. Of course, U.S. exports fell and imports rose.

Moreover, the rise in the interest rate set in motion a self-fueled speculative rise in both the dollar and in the prices of U.S. securities. The rise in the dollar led people to buy the dollar, expecting the rise to continue. Similarly the long rise in the Dow average led people to buy securities as though there was no ceiling. By late 1985 the real interest rate in the United States was no longer higher than it was abroad. When the central bankers of the Group of Five— West Germany, France, the UK, Japan, and the United States— decided at the Plaza Hotel that enough was enough, the dollar was being held up only by expectations of further increases.

The Fed decided that the dollar had gone high enough: enough auto, steel, textile, and apparel workers were out of work. The flow of imports had reached a high enough level, and exports were lower than even the Fed could tolerate. Although the economy generally was prosperous late in 1985, in parts of the country high unemployment persisted. Unskilled workers suffered the worst effects of the Fed's severe anti-inflation policy. Formerly highly-paid factory workers were either unemployed or took low-paid jobs as counter clerks in fast-food drive-ins. Not surprisingly, Richard Gephardt's protectionist bill was gaining support in Congress. The Fed's policy had exported jobs. The high U.S. interest rate and the dollar's climb were blessings to other countries. The only way Congress could counter the employment effects of the Fed's monetary tightness was to raise protectionist barriers against imports. Gephardt's bill did not pass, but the protectionist sentiment remains strong.

The consequences of the tight monetary policy for the dollar and for trade were totally unexpected. A tight monetary policy was expected to drive down demand, including the demand for imports, not raise the dollar and therefore imports. Nor was it supposed to hurt exports. The theory underlying the monetary policy did not predict that it would benefit foreign workers at the cost of domestic workers. What the Fed ignored was the effect of a high U.S. interest rate on investment and the speculative demand for the dollar.

The Fed, along with other central banks, realized that the continued ascent of the dollar would provoke a quick buildup by the United States of import barriers and the destruction of the General Agreement on Tariffs and Trade (GATT), under which the participating countries had reduced tariffs in the sixties and seventies, promoting a huge growth in world trade. The central banks began to sell the dollar to drive down its price. Success came quickly because by this time the dollar was being supported only by thin expectational reeds.

Once the turn came, the dollar continued its fall. The central bankers met in February 1987 at the Louvre in Paris. They agreed that the descent had gone far enough. The Bundesbank, the Bank of Japan, and the Bank of England pressed the Fed to do its part by tightening the supply of money and raising the interest rate. They also demanded that the United States cut the federal budget deficit. The foreign central banks had been supporting the dollar with their purchases throughout 1986, and as it continued to fall their losses mounted. As buyers in any falling market, they were anxious to get out. But they could not now recover their original investment by selling dollars with foreign exchange rates as low as they were. Their losses would grow as the foreign exchange rates fell further and as they continued to buy more dollars. If the dollar was not to fall any further and the central banks were to discontinue their support, then the U.S. interest rate had to rise relative to interest rates abroad. The trade deficit showed no sign of falling. The dollar had to be maintained by encouraging foreign investment in the United States.

The agreement committed foreign central banks to pursue easier monetary policies. If the Bundesbank reduced the rate of interest in West Germany, business investment and consumer spending would increase. Unemployment was high, partly as a result of the severe antiinflation policy pursued by the central bank. An easier monetary policy would stimulate employment. The inflation rate in West Germany was only about 1 percent, so the Bundesbank would not be taking great risks. An easier monetary policy would raise the West German demand for dollars by stimulating investment and consumption and thus imports from the United States. The dollar would also gain some strength from the resulting fall in the interest rate in West Germany. Investors would shift from West German securities to U.S. securities. Japan made similar promises. Japan risked little inflation by pursuing a stimulative policy. Although the unemployment rate was low, the inflation rate was zero.

For the United States, Treasury Secretary Baker promised that the budget deficit would be reduced by $70 billion. Foreign finance ministers and central bankers demanded that the United States reduce the budget deficit, expecting that this would bring the dollar's fall to a halt. However, there was no reason to expect a deficit reduction to have this effect. What was important was the real interest rate in the United States relative to the real interest rate in other countries. Only if the real rate in the United States rose relative to foreign real rates would the dollar rise. But a smaller budget deficit would have the opposite effect. It would tend to reduce the U.S. real interest rate by cutting the demand for credit by the federal government. Thus, the fact that Reagan did not back up Baker's promise did not cause the dollar to continue its downward course.

Although the Fed did not promise to support the dollar by raising the interest rate, it did tighten the money supply. On the other hand, as we can see in Table 5.1, Japan and West Germany did not cut their interest rates. They excused their failure to fulfill their commitments by pointing to the United States' failure to cut the deficit. In West Germany the money market rate remained the same between February and September. In Japan it fell by only .2 percentage points. They persisted despite Baker's threats to allow the dollar to fall further. However, they did support the dollar by active intervention in foreign exchange markets. In the first half of 1987 foreign central banks bought 23.4 billion U.S. dollars. The Fed contributed by raising the U.S. rate of interest. The table shows that the Fed raised the U.S. short-term rate of interest by as much as 1.1 percentage points. We have already seen the effect of the Fed's policy on the long-term rate.

Table 5.1
Short-Term Money Market Rates in
the United States, Japan, and West Germany,
February and September 1987 (percentages)

	February	September
United States	6.10	7.22
Japan	3.98	3.77
West Germany	3.94	3.98

Sources: Federal Reserve Bulletin, November 1987, p. A67; ibid., February 1988, p. A67; *Economic Report of the President 1988,* pp. 330–31.

Note: U.S. federal funds rate. Other rates are three-month interbank loan rates.

The dollar's continued descent upset both the Fed and the Treasury because it threatened to add to inflationary pressures. Although the overall unemployment rate still was as high as 5.9 percent, it was lower than at any time since 1979, and some occupational labor shortages might set off a wage–price spiral. In addition, a lower dollar would raise import prices.

THE FED POLICY AND THE CRASH

The Fed did not expect its policy to have so devastating an effect on stock prices. Volcker and Greenspan did not take a calculated risk of shrinking the wealth of the people who had their savings invested in pension funds, mutual funds, and directly in stocks. They probably were not willing to take even a 10 percent risk of a great fall in the stock market to maintain the value of the dollar, especially since Secretary Baker was willing to see a further decline in the dollar. Unwittingly, Volcker and Greenspan pushed up the interest rate; they failed to recognize how vulnerable the stock market was. The Fed undertook a policy of extreme monetary tightness out of ignorance of the consequences for the market.

Although the Fed was charged with maintaining economic stability, it was no wiser than the ordinary investors who had chased stock prices up nearly 40 percent over the previous year. Volcker and Greenspan were caught up in the same speculative mania as everyone else. Most economists also went along. Many agreed with the optimistic market forecasters who ascribed the rise to the earlier general inflation. Stock market prices were not yet as high as the values of assets, which had risen in the seventies. To build the physical plant of the companies listed would have cost much more than to buy their stocks. This undervaluation of underlying assets motivated many of the takeovers preceding the crash. However, the judgment that stock market prices were low overlooked a more fundamental consideration—earnings. The Fed along with everyone else ignored the historically high levels of stock price/earnings ratios and the low dividend yields. Just before the crash the Standard and Poor's 500-stock price/earnings ratio had reached the level of 22, which was much higher than the level of 16 reached the previous year. The average dividend yield was down to 2.8 percent, compared to 3.4 percent the previous year. Nevertheless, the Fed persisted in raising the rate of interest.

Immediately following the crash the Fed reversed direction to prop up the stock market. The crash frightened the Fed into putting a flood of money into the banking system. In the three short weeks between October 21 and November 11, it raised the banking system's excess reserves from $976 million to $1,517 million; net free reserves went up from $485 million to $1,232 million. As a result, the federal funds rate fell sharply from 7.48 to 6.73 percent.

The central banks of West Germany, France and the Netherlands also were frightened. They announced a reduction in their discount rates, relieving some of the pressure on the Fed to support the dollar. Nevertheless, by March 1988 the dollar fell another 7 percent against the German mark and 12 percent against the yen. To prevent the slide from getting any worse, the Fed resumed its tight monetary policy. It succeeded in stopping the fall.

THE FUTURE

Wary of both inflation and of a continuing drop in the dollar, the Fed is unlikely to allow the real interest rate to fall any further. The policy risks bringing on a recession. High interest costs have cut housing starts and are likely to reduce total investment. The Fed is walking a narrow path between inflation and recession.

The standoff on the budget deficit does not help. If Congress and the administration were to reach an agreement that cut the deficit by a significant amount—say by $100 billion—then the real interest rate could come down without precipitating inflation. The Fed would find it easier to maintain a tight monetary policy.

A fall in the real interest rate would stem the flow of foreign capital into the United States, cutting the demand for the dollar. The trade deficit can be expected to fall with the dollar. Additional taxes will reduce income available for spending and thus imports.

CONCLUSION

Again, the deficit was not the villain. The stock market crashed because the Fed tried to maintain the value of the dollar by raising the interest rate. It pursued an extremely tight monetary policy, one that was unhealthy for the fragile stock market. The Fed was unaware of the likely disastrous consequences. We see here another example of the ignorance with which policymakers conduct economic policy. Congress has entrusted a large measure of economic policy to the Fed, expecting it to be well informed, objective, and wise. Instead, we find that it carried out an extreme policy out of ignorance of some basic economic relationships.

6
THE DECLINE OF MANUFACTURING EMPLOYMENT

Suffering from foreign competition, the auto, steel, textile, apparel, and other industries continue to demand protection against imports. The United Auto Workers, the United Steelworkers, and the Amalgamated Clothing and Textile Workers join together with Ford, Chrysler, USX, and Burlington Industries to demand protection against imports. Political leaders in such depressed areas as Louisiana, West Virginia, and Mississippi make the same demands. The unions add the demand for low-cost loans for manufacturers. Felix Rohatyn supports this demand by proposing a development bank on the model of the Reconstruction Finance Corporation (RFC) of the thirties.

Some economists, like Lester Thurow and Robert Reich, also urge such assistance. To avoid violating the canons of economics, they refrain from laying it on the line by calling for protection against imports or for subsidies; rather, they euphemistically propose an industrial policy. They envision support for rising industries, with rosy economic prospects, neglecting to mention the part of an industrial policy that will protect declining industries.

The reality is that steel, textiles, autos, and apparel are the industries that will receive protection and assistance. Economic schemes do not carry the day in Washington. Political clout is what matters, and senators and members of Congress do not have to worry about the voters working in nonexistent or small industries. A defense of an industrial policy that views the federal government as the knowledgeable grand planner, selecting industries with great hopes, will merely hide the true objective, which will be to preserve existing jobs in declining industries.

CONTINUING HIGH UNEMPLOYMENT AND THE DECLINE OF MANUFACTURING

For the many still unemployed the high prosperity has been a myth. It is the professional and managerial workers in rapidly growing industries like hospitals and computer services who have enjoyed full employment at high wages, not the floor cleaners in factories manufacturing farm tractors. The total unemployment rate of only 5.0 percent is deceptive, for it covers computer architects and corporate lawyers who do not have to worry about jobs, along with those whose jobs are insecure. Therefore, the overall rate understates the incidence of unemployment among unskilled factory workers. In March 1989 as many as 11.6 percent of handlers, equipment cleaners, helpers, and laborers were unemployed.[1] In other words, on any day that month on the average nearly one out of every nine persons in this large category was unemployed.

The figures on unemployment even among the unskilled understate the extent of unemployment in this group because part-time workers are counted as employed, even though many hold such jobs because they cannot find full-time jobs. They are not even counted as partly unemployed.

Even if we were to ignore the part-timers, the rate for the unskilled does not reveal how bad things are for them. The Census Bureau drops those from the count of the unemployed who give up waiting in lines at employment offices. If you want to be counted part of the labor force by the statisticians, you have either to have a job or to be looking for one. Including these jobless persons would raise the unemployment rate several percentage points.

In addition, unemployment strikes many more workers at some time during the year than the average for a month or even for a year indicates. Many more than one out of nine unskilled workers lose their jobs and find others during the year, or are laid off and rehired. A much larger proportion of the labor force is unemployed part of the year than the average percentage for the year.

Things are worse for some regions and some groups than the

figures indicate. The 11.6 percent unemployment rate is the national rate. West Virginia, Louisiana, and Mississippi have been hit harder than most states. In addition, as is well known, some demographic groups, most notably young blacks, have suffered greatly.

If we try to locate the source of the unemployment, we will notice at once the loss of jobs in manufacturing. Here I refer to absolute numbers, not to manufacturing's share of total employment. Even a slow rate of growth of employment in manufacturing entails the loss of jobs. Unless the number of jobs in manufacturing grows as fast as the labor force, or, given a slow rate of growth in manufacturing, other sectors grow more rapidly than the labor force, unemployment will increase. Despite prosperity, employment in manufacturing has actually fallen—not just grown slowly. Between 1980 and 1987 employment in that sector fell as much as 6 percent.[2] True, the number of jobs has grown elsewhere. There are more waiters, hospital orderlies, and retail clerks than in 1980. In all industries taken together, the number of jobs rose by 13 percent.[3] Nevertheless, a high level of unemployment has persisted, and one of the reasons has been the decline in the number of unskilled jobs in manufacturing.

Because of the growth of other sectors, not all of the unskilled former manufacturing workers are unemployed. In 1986 services, including hotels, barber and beauty shops, repair services, business services, laundries, and so on, employed 24 percent more people than in 1980. Retailers and wholesalers employed 16 percent more. Services now employ more people than manufacturing does; retailers and wholesalers also are more important.[4]

But those who lost their jobs in manufacturing and found jobs elsewhere have little cause for joy. They suffered substantial cuts in pay. In 1986 the average annual total compensation, including all benefits, of full-time employees who worked year-round in manufacturing was $31,219. The comparable figure for services was $22,307, and for retail trade it was $16,183.[5] Many former manufacturing workers had to move down from a middle-class income and standard of living to near poverty.

THE JAPAN MODEL

The AFL-CIO, the Cuomo Commission, Thurow, Reich, and other proponents of an industrial policy say that U.S. manufacturing is in decline. The abandoned steel mills in the Monongahela Valley are examples of what is called the deindustrialization of America. In the 1984 election campaign, Walter Mondale's crystal ball showed a nation of hamburger flippers working under the sign of the big M. Manufacturing has been associated with production and therefore with economic and military strength. The services and retailing sectors are hardly adequate substitutes. The industrial policy advocates unknowingly agree with the Soviets and the Marxists in rejecting the service and distribution industries as unproductive. True production industries include only agriculture, mining, and manufacturing. The transformation of materials into valuable goods qualifies as production, not the distribution of those goods, nor services.

Naturally, the AFL-CIO and its xenophobic supporters blame the alleged decline of manufacturing on foreigners, particularly the Japanese. They watch with envy the enormous growth of Japan's manufacturing output and exports. As long as Americans could boast about their far superior incomes and standard of living while the Japanese lived in Asiatic poverty, there was no reason to envy them. But in the postwar period the standard of living of the Japanese has gone from less than half that of Americans to near equality. We can no longer pride ourselves on American genius, innovation, skills, education, ways of life, freedom, or whatever it is that raises productivity. The galling thing is that the Japanese are as good, if not better, at production, which used to be what we prided ourselves on most. So high a value did we place on economic success that we cannot now rate ourselves according to cultural or spiritual values.

Congressman Gephardt, among others, sees the Japanese as vicious competitors who keep American goods out of the home market by relying on unfair trade practices. They do not play by the rules of the game, as set by the General Agreement on Tariffs and Trade (GATT). Thus, the Japanese buy only their own telecommunications equipment for their telephone system, refusing to look at competitive U.S. products.

Thurow and Reich see the Japanese in a more favorable light. The secret of Japanese success is superior productivity due to worker-management cooperation. U.S. businesses should imitate the winners in the world competition for exports by inviting workers to participate in quality circles, where they can discuss with management ways to improve productivity. Apparently, however, it took more than quality circles and soliciting workers' participation to build up Japanese industry. Thurow and Reich, among others, urge policymakers to follow the example of Japan by pursuing an industrial policy. Japan's industrial policy receives much of the credit for the economic miracle. The lesson that is drawn is that to compete, the United States will have to adopt one, too.

The proponents of an industrial policy modeled after the Japanese industrial policy do not tell us how much competition has been controlled in Japan. "Industrial policy" is a vague, uninformative phrase. Thurow and Reich tell us little about the Japanese policy beyond referring to subsidies and protection. The government through the Ministry of International Trade and Industry (MITI) encouraged the formation of cartels in the favored industries. The full story would make the Japanese industrial policy less attractive as a model.

Immediately after its defeat in World War II, Japan embarked on a policy of industrial development. The government set out to accelerate the growth of large firms in favored industries, which at one time or another included steel, radios and televisions, other electronic products, machine tools, semiconductors, and automobiles. The recipients of the assistance had such familiar names as Matsushita, Mitsubishi, and Hitachi. After the war credit was in short supply. The local banks channeled savings to the Bank of Japan, which made loans to the favored firms at low rates of interest. Small businesses were starved for credit. The mom and pop stores, which predominate in retailing, could not finance their inventories. In fact, unlike manufacturing, retailing in Japan is still today quite primitive by U.S. standards. The major manufacturers, who could draw on the nation's capital, had to supply the retailers with credit.

The home market was protected in a variety of ways. Foreign manufacturers could not gain access to wholesalers or retailers, financed by domestic manufacturers. Tied by financial and other strings to Matsushita, the electronic products retailer would not for a moment entertain the thought of selling a Zenith product. New businesses that might have introduced foreign goods into the market could not obtain financing from the highly centralized banking system. Moreover, customs inspectors zealously enforced safety and other regulations that also kept foreign products out of the home market.

Shielded against imports, the manufacturers cheerfully colluded to set home market prices. Matsushita's managers met regularly in the best hotels with Hitachi's, Sharp's, Mitsubishi's, and other managers. American managers behaving the same way would soon have found themselves in jail. But the Japanese managers had no such fears. True, the Japanese have an antitrust law. But the Diet passed the law under the hoof of the U.S. military occupation authorities. As soon as the occupation was over the Diet removed whatever teeth the law had. The courts never enforced the law. The following discussion of the operations of cartels is based on information collected in the antitrust case, *Matsushita Electric Industrial Co. Ltd. et al. v. Zenith Radio Corp. et al.*, which described the collusive activities of the television and electronic products manufacturers.[6] Since many of these manufacturers also are active in other markets, it is unlikely that the collusion in the television and electronics products markets was peculiar. Moreover, other writers have argued that price collusion has been widespread in Japanese industry.

The agreements were worked out very thoroughly. The conspirators met often and regularly enough to leave no loophole open for competition. Since the Japanese experience with cartels goes back a long way—there were cartels as far back as the twenties and possibly earlier—the manufacturers knew that competition might break out if any one of them produced too much, accumulated inventories, or had excess capacity. Accordingly, representatives of the manufacturers met regularly to exchange information on outputs and sales.

They also knew that unless they set retail as well as manufacturing prices, competition might break out. A special group of manfacturers' representatives met regularly to regulate retail competition. The restrictions at the retail level guarded against secret discounts, and they set retail as well as their own wholesale prices. When necessary, the agreements went into great detail to describe the various products.

Negotiations relating to manufacturers' prices were conducted at frequent meetings of middle management groups. In the television industry there were the Tenth Day group, the Television Study group, the MD group, and others. When an impasse was reached, the disagreement was passed on to senior management groups. These included the Palace group, consisting of high-ranking officials, and the Okura group, consisting of the top executives.

With a protected home market to exploit, the Japanese manufacturers could underprice their foreign competitors. The high prices in the home market provided the manufacturers with a cushion of profits from which they could draw while losing money on foreign sales.

The manufacturers did not limit their conspiracy to the domestic market. They knew that if competition broke out among themselves in foreign markets, they would find it difficult to maintain the conspiracy at home. The television manufacturers had built up a capacity to supply foreign as well as domestic markets, and if one of them suffered from excess capacity as a result of a loss of foreign sales, that company might be tempted to expand its sales in the home market by cutting prices. The agreements covering foreign markets prohibited manufacturers from taking foreign customers away from one another as well as price competition. A series of groups, paralleling those conspiring to control prices in the home market, met regularly to negotiate agreements for foreign markets.

MITI actively participated in the development of what were essentially cartels. It encouraged cooperation among the manufacturers, applying pressure to individual companies that were dissatisfied with their share of sales and persisted in competing. Moreover, it selected the industries and the firms to be favored with low-cost credit. MITI undertook to direct the development of Japanese industry.

The essential features of the policy were low-cost credit to a selected list of firms in selected industries, a closed home market for these industries, price collusion in the home market and among the Japanese manufacturers abroad, and underpricing non-Japanese competitors in foreign markets. Thus the Japanese industrial policy did not only consist of subsidies to firms in the targeted industries and of protection of the home market. It included carefully negotiated and vigorously enforced price agreements.

The emphasis on Japan's industrial policy obscures the role of the other elements in that country's economic development. Merely by following Japan's precedent, even to the extent of controlling competition, which the U.S. is unlikely to tolerate, does not assure success. The Japanese have many well-trained engineers and technicians, and workers generally are well educated. In addition, labor and management live together more harmoniously than in the United States. The companies have a patriarchal relationship with their workers. Employment is guaranteed. Much of the compensation received by the workers takes the form of an annual bonus, which is based on profits. Social life is organized around the companies. As a result, the unions are much weaker than in the United States. We could add to this list of general social factors aiding Japan's economic growth.

Perhaps because the contribution of low wages to Japan's economic success is obvious, it receives less notice than the industrial policy or labor-management cooperation. In any case, the AFL–CIO is not keen to have wages reduced, and even the Cuomo Commission was unprepared to make such a recommendation. Over most of the postwar period Japanese manufacturers paid much lower wages than U.S. workers received. Because labor continued to flow from rural to urban areas as late as the seventies, much after rural migration had ceased in the West, the supply of labor to manufacturing was plentiful. Wages remained much below Western levels. In recent years, as labor costs have mounted, Japanese manufacturers have shifted their production, much as U.S. manufacturers have done, to South Korea and Taiwan, where wages are much lower than in Japan.

AN AMERICAN INDUSTRIAL POLICY

In its call for an industrial policy, the AFL–CIO did not dare urge the formation of cartels on the Japanese model. Nevertheless, raising or even maintaining employment in depressed industries is a hopeless goal without cartels.

The AFL–CIO does not even pretend to support the principles of free trade. It does not say that protection is needed only temporarily while industries that have been badly hit by foreign competition recover. Without mincing words, the AFL–CIO rejects economic arguments for free trade as theoretical. The organization calls for protection generally, and more specifically for the auto, steel, textile, apparel, aircraft, copper, machine tool, telecommunications products, printing, and maritime industries. This is a pretty long list. The unions in these industries must swing more weight than those representing the workers in the aircraft and machinery industries, whose jobs depend on exports. If Congress abandons GATT and protects the industries in the AFL–CIO's list, other countries will retaliate, and our export industries will suffer.

Protection was not enough for the AFL–CIO. It also demanded a development bank to invest public funds in reindustrialization projects. We hear a similar proposal from Rohatyn, who urges a new Reconstruction Finance Corporation (RFC), which President Roosevelt set up to assist depressed industries in the thirties. The new RFC would select industries and companies to be assisted. The projects would be part of what the AFL–CIO organization called an industrial policy.

An interesting aspect of the AFL–CIO's proposal is that the projects in each industry would be administered by labor-management-government committees. The committee for the steel industry would include representatives of the United Steelworkers, the companies, and the government. This committee presumably would decide which firms would obtain the assistance.

The Cuomo Commission on Trade and Competitiveness went further than the AFL–CIO in calling for the regulation of competition. It too proposed labor-management-government committees to administer the industrial policy in each industry. But it was much more specific about what the committees would do. The commission called for the development of long-term trade strategies on the basis of economic studies by labor-management-government task forces. To be sure, industries queuing up for subsidies will have to show how they plan to improve their competitiveness. The assistance given to Chrysler will be a forerunner of many more such instances in other industries.

Asserting that world overcapacity afflicts many industries, the report recommended market-sharing agreements to prevent destructive competition. The commission evidently recognized that subsidies and import restrictions would not be enough to raise employment in individual industries; cartel-like agreements also would be necessary. The participants would attempt to maintain employment without engaging in price-cutting competition. Past efforts to organize cartels in the United States have been justified by the threat of destructive competition brought about by overcapacity. In general, the antitrust laws have been interpreted as prohibiting such cartels. In Japan, by contrast, the government has promoted cartels. One of the justifications has been overcapacity and the threat of destructive competition. The commission was recommending the abandonment of competition in what may be a large part of manufacturing for the same reason that past cartel organizers have cited.

When countries negotiate agreements, they have a wider reach than when private companies do. Governments must look out for more than the interests of companies in a single industry. Thus, measures to protect industries competing with imports may result in retaliatory measures by other countries against that country's exports. The Japanese might retaliate against reductions in U.S. import quotas for autos and steel by restricting imports of wheat, beef, and aircraft. Agreements might have to be extended to a large number of markets.

Administering such agreements would be no easy matter. A U.S. agency would have to allocate the export quotas among the sellers in each market. Which U.S. textile manufacturers would have the right to export? How much would each one be allowed to export? Market-sharing agreements presumably would be based on the participants' historical shares of various markets. New manufacturers would be prohibited from exporting, and small firms' exports could not grow. Firms in industries operating under market-sharing agreements would not be able to compete vigorously with one another in export markets. There would be little point to price competition, since the sales would be limited.

The new administration may be attracted by the proposal to enter into agreements covering foreign markets with the governments of other countries. American companies will find it difficult to compete in the world market with Japanese companies backed by their government, monopolistically exploiting a home market, and pursuing low-price policies to increase their market shares. This is one of the justifications currently being offered by proponents of an industrial policy for market-sharing agreements. Moreover, such international agreements are permitted by the Webb-Pomerene Export Trade Act of 1918.

However, the agreements will have to extend to the home market. No purpose would be served to have the agreements cover foreign markets while leaving the U.S. market open to foreign companies without any control over market shares. The United States is the largest market by far for American companies, and it is hardly inconsequential for major foreign companies. We have gone part of the way down this road by negotiating Voluntary Restraint Agreements (VRAs) with Japan and South Korea covering automobiles and steel. The pressures for such agreements are so powerful that even the Reagan administration, committed though it was to liberalizing trade, was forced to enter into them.

A fully-developed industrial policy would have to set domestic prices and wages as well. When only a few domestic sellers compete for sales, they might succeed in raising prices in the United States. Once the Japanese are restricted to part of the market, the U.S. companies would not have to fear being undercut in price, which, after all, would be the purpose of the agreements. The VRAs have already had this effect in autos and steel.

We cannot count on the policy protecting consumers' interests. A government agency is likely to set high prices. The problem is that an industrial policy is intended to protect producers—workers and management. The basic purpose is to preserve employment opportunities by protecting markets, not to provide consumers with goods at low prices.

That this is so can also be seen in the proposal by both the Cuomo Commission and the AFL–CIO that a labor-management-government committee administer the industrial policy in each market. The government supposedly would guard consumers' interests. But the government will be more sensitive to the more focused, stronger interests of producers. Those who earn their incomes from a particular industry will fight much more vigorously than consumers, for whom expenditures for the products of that industry make up a small percentage of their total expenditures. As we know, politicians depend on trade associations and unions to finance their election campaigns, not consumer groups. In any case, the direct representation of labor and management in the committees will heavily weight their decisions.

Cartelization, market-sharing agreements, and price and wage controls are unlikely to provide long-run solutions. They may worsen the basic economic condition of the industries. High prices, which encouraged the building of new capacity in steel and automobiles, among other products, were the source of the overcapacity and the destructive competition. The intention of the industrial policy would be to protect the high prices. I have mentioned the effects of the VRA on car prices. Before the Japanese agreed to limit their exports the industry had been cutting costs and prices. When the U.S. industry's market share was assured, the pressure was off. Costs were allowed to rise, and prices followed.

It does not take much profound thought to realize that for the plans to be more than scraps of paper, firms would have to agree to production quotas, capacity limits, investment, as well as prices and wages. The proposals smack of Roosevelt's NRA and fascist corporatism without the excuse of the Great Depression. Ruling the industries, the government-management-labor committees, of course, would favor producers', not consumers', interests. Competition would be tightly restrained.

THE CASE FOR AN INDUSTRIAL POLICY

We are asked to believe that the economy, particularly manufacturing, has been performing not just badly but dreadfully. Otherwise why abandon competition even in only a few industries? Advocates for an industrial policy point to the fall in manufacturing employment. Although the need for such a policy hardly seems urgent now that unemployment in the country as a whole has dropped to its lowest level in 15 years, unskilled workers continue to suffer, and parts of the country have not recovered. Moreover, former auto assembly workers now working as dishwashers have little to cheer about.

Suppose we agree that manufacturing needs a revitalizing injection. That alone does not justify the abandonment of competition. We need a diagnosis of the illness and a convincing argument that the proposed remedy will cure it. The economic doctors tell us that the sad performance is due to the loss of markets, which has several causes. I have already mentioned the complaints about Japan's and South Korea's unfair trade practices, other countries' barriers to imports, and Japan's industrial policy.

Industrial policy proponents also point to slow productivity growth. U.S. manufacturing has lost the efficiency race to Japan and possibly to other countries. As always, productivity growth is the great hope. It is the manna from heaven that will pay for everything and permit us to avoid choices. The efficiency argument also provides the satisfaction of fixing blame for the problems on management and labor. Management has been lazy and has allowed costs to creep up. Unions have demanded work rules that waste labor. These generalizations usually can be fleshed out with anecdotes describing instances of inefficiency that appear to support the conclusion of rampant waste. Apparently, competition has not been lively in the American economy—much less lively than in Japan. The generalizations about inefficiency have much more appeal than economic discussions of the effects of high exchange rates for the dollar.

High wages receive attention but understandably cannot be blamed. Wages cannot be cut to the Korean level.

Of course, productivity and wages are not the whole story. The phenomenal rise of the dollar between 1980 and 1985 did some damage. To overcome the effects of an increase of 56 percent in the value of the dollar would take a wopping increase in efficiency. Many economists, among others, blame the budget deficit for the dollar's rise. However, if the deficits are the deadly virus, then an industrial policy is hardly the cure.

The case relies on Japan's unfair trade practices. The model, Japan, protects its workers against unemployment by restricting imports and subsidizing the exports of the large Japanese manufacturers with low-cost financing. MITI devised and monitors the overall plan. To catch up we have to imitate the current winner. Our planners should be able to do as well as the Japanese planners.

Much of the discussion takes the form of descriptions of Japanese import barriers. Foreign manufacturers of electronic products cannot overcome barriers created on the pretext of safety regulations. The telecommunications products market is restricted to domestic producers. American manufacturers generally cannot gain access to the distribution system. We also hear about MITI's subsidies to large manufacturers. We read many stories. The inference is drawn that the U.S. government must support American manufacturers if they are to compete effectively in the world market. These arguments do not address the issue of the effectiveness of U.S. manufacturing competition as a whole. Selective anecdotes prove nothing. Of course, some industries will decline, but others will rise. To dwell on a few dying industries is misleading.

How effective U.S. competition in manufacturing as a whole is is the critical issue. The question of whether or not U.S. telecommunications products manufacturers are competing on a level field with Japanese manufacturers does not deal with the overall issue. One can always find examples of unfair competition. Such examples do not justify government intervention into markets on a wide scale. We should know how well manufacturing as a whole has performed. Addressing this general issue entails evaluating the growth of output in relation to employment, the growth of productivity, the part played in the growth of output by the growth of the domestic market, as well as the growth of exports and of imports.

THE PERFORMANCE OF MANUFACTURING

Some elementary questions have yet to be answered. The proposition that the loss of markets to foreign producers has caused the observed rise in unemployment and shift to low-paid employment raises the question: How fast has the output of American manufacturing been growing? If American manufacturing has not competed effectively, then the output of the manufacturing sector has not grown rapidly enough to keep the labor force employed. The objective is a high rate of employment at high wages. Manufacturing gets all the attention because it is the high-wage sector of the economy.

Presumably, the growth rate of this sector's output was less than the growth rate of the total labor force. We keep reading about unemployed auto and steel workers who were driven out of their jobs by foreigners who relied on unfair practices and an industrial policy. The implication is that manufacturing employment has grown too slowly to keep a growing labor force employed at high wages, and the cause has been a slow rate of growth of output. The lack of an industrial policy has given the advantage to the rapacious Japanese.

But this is all fiction. Manufacturing output has not grown slowly; it has grown rapidly in relation to the labor force. Between

1980 and 1987 real GNP in manufacturing grew much faster than the total labor force. The growth rate of manufacturing output was 3.4 percent[7] compared to 1.6 percent for the total labor force.[8] These numbers show that markets have been growing rapidly enough. So much for the loss-of-markets diagnosis.

THE IMPORTANCE OF MANUFACTURING

Should we believe the popular view that manufacturing is declining in importance—that the United States is becoming a service economy? We keep hearing that manufacturing is a disappearing part of the American economy. True, manufacturing employment has fallen and the labor force has not stopped growing. Over the short six years between 1980 and 1986, manufacturing employment fell from 22.4 percent of the total to 19.1 percent. Since it is part of a long trend, the drop can be expected to continue. The falling trend in this share began long before 1980. In 1960 manufacturing accounted for 31 percent of total U.S. employment.

Why the concern? For managers, professionals, and office workers, it makes little difference whether they work in service or in manufacturing industries. The lawyer who works at Sears' head office does as well as the one who works for Boeing. However, for unskilled materials handlers in factories, it matters. Manufacturing has paid higher wages than service industries. For them, a shift into the service industries generally means a loss of income.

We have to understand the source of the decline in manufacturing's share of employment. The call for a radical remedy diagnoses the source as a fall in output. So let us look at output. We have seen that manufacturing output has grown. The diagnosis suggests that manufacturing output has fallen relative to the output of the rest of the economy. But this, too, is false. Manufacturing output has grown faster than the output of the rest of the economy. Between 1980 and 1986 the rate of growth of manufacturing output was 3.3 percent, which was much higher than the 2.3 percent rate for the other sectors. Manufacturing's share of total output has grown. Measured in constant (1982) dollars, manufacturing's share of the GNP increased from 20.9 to 21.9 percent between 1980 and 1986. This relative growth of output also is part of a long trend.[9]

The obvious explanation for the decline in manufacturing employment is rapid productivity growth. Productivity, which we shall discuss later, has grown at a much faster rate in manufacturing than in the other sectors. Those who bewail America's loss of competitiveness, to which they attribute the decline of manufacturing employment, call for improvements in productivity. The argument is that employment has suffered because U.S. businesses have lost markets to their more efficient Japanese competitors. If they are to regain these markets, U.S. manufacturers will have to accelerate their productivity growth. But it is not slow but rapid productivity growth that accounts for the decline in manufacturing employment. Manufacturing did not lose sales measured in constant dollars, so the loss of employment was not at all due to the loss of markets. As we will see, all of the loss of employment was due to productivity growth and to more hours worked per employee.

The confusion is due partly to the greater prominence of current-dollar GNP measures of the importance of different sectors. The GNP figures that we usually see are not corrected for price changes; they measure output in current, not in constant dollars. Current-dollar GNP measures not only fail to reveal the the growing percentage of total output supplied by manufacturing, but show a negative trend. Between 1980 and 1986 in current dollars this percentage fell from 21.3 to 19.5 percent. That is to say, measured in 1980 prices, manufacturing output accounted for 21.3 percent of total output in 1980. Measured in 1986 prices, manufacturing output accounted for 19.3 percent in 1986.

Here we have another discrepancy to account for. Again, productivity growth is the link. Rapid productivity growth caused manufactured goods prices to fall relative to the prices of services, which make up the bulk of the rest of the economy. Efficiency gains meant reductions in costs. In our generally competitive economy, reductions in costs over a long enough period result in price cuts. The consumer gains the benefits. To take a prominent example, the office machinery industry could produce microcomputers with less labor in 1986 than in 1980. The technology was advancing rapidly—more rapidly than in other economic sectors. As a result, the prices of PCs fell while prices of other products were rising in the continuing general inflation.

Rapid productivity growth is the reason the constant-dollar output figures for manufacturing show an increase while the current-dollar figures show a decline. The volume of output has grown, even though the current-dollar measure of GNP, which reflects price reductions, does not reveal the growth. Productivity growth reduces costs and therefore prices. Since manufacturing has enjoyed faster productivity growth than other sectors, prices have come down more. The relative decline of manufacturing prices results in the appearance of a decline in the consumption of manufactured goods relative to services. But we are not consuming a bigger bundle of laundry services, restaurant meals, repair services, and medical services, taken together, relative to the bundle of appliances, apparel, cars, processed foods, and other manufactured products. We do spend more of our incomes on services relative to manufactured goods now than before. But this is because the prices of services have gone up more, not because services have become more important. The constant-dollar measures of output, which hold prices constant, show the true growth of relative outputs of the two sectors.

THE EFFECT OF PRODUCTIVITY GROWTH ON EMPLOYMENT

Not only has manufacturing's share of total employment fallen, but the absolute number of persons employed in this sector has declined. Between 1980 and 1987 employment fell at the rate of 0.8 percent.[10]

Again, assuming that the decline is symptomatic of some disease, we have to know the cause before we can prescribe a remedy. Industrial policy proponents pray for higher productivity, which they hope will raise manufacturing's competitiveness and therefore employment. The diagnosis blames the inferior efficiency of U.S. manufacturing.

One reason employment fell is very simple and has nothing to do with efficiency. Labor input is measured more accurately as labor hours, which fell at the lesser rate of 0.4 percent.[11] Accordingly, hours worked per worker increased at the rate of 0.4 percent. Thus, part of the decline in employment was due to the rise in hours worked per worker. The explanation of the rise in hours is that some costs rise more with the number of workers than with the number of hours worked. These include hiring and training costs and employers' contributions to the costs of medical insurance.

Of course, output grew while labor hours fell because productivity advanced. So, productivity growth may be the source of the ill—the fall in manufacturing employment—not the remedy, industrial policy proponents to the contrary. "Productivity" here refers to labor productivity. Productivity grew at a very rapid rate— 3.8 percent[12]—the difference between the growth rates of output and labor hours (3.4 percent minus −0.4 percent). Indeed, the growth in productivity was so rapid that we can say that it was chiefly responsible for the fall in employment.

Part of the improvement was due to the substitution of plant and machinery for labor. While manufacturers employ less and less labor, they continue to augment their capital equipment. However, in the eighties the displacement of labor by capital was much less than in the seventies. The growth rate of the net capital stock, 1.3 percent, was much less than in the seventies, when it was 3.2 percent.[13] Nevertheless, the capital stock grew while labor input fell.

Thus, one of the reasons for the gain in productivity and the fall in employment in manufacturing has been the growing use of buildings, machinery, and equipment. The relative growth in the employment of capital equipment in the eighties continues the long trend. Between 1950 and 1987 the quantity of capital employed per worker in manufacturing more than doubled.

We tend to take the growth of capital stock per worker for granted, as though it is one of the laws of nature that plants will become increasingly automated. As knowledge and technology advance, manufacturers employ more equipment per worker. Advancing technology may have contributed to the greater utilization of capital per worker. However, it is also true that over the postwar period wages have increased enormously relative to the cost of machinery and equipment, inducing manufacturers to automate production processes. Between 1950 and 1987 real hourly compensation, which includes fringe benefits, doubled.[14] By contrast, the real interest rate fell by one quarter. In some years of the seventies the real rate was negative owing to the high rate of inflation. Over the same period the purchase price of machinery and capital equipment generally fell relative to prices generally. Productivity growth in the machinery industries has been more rapid than the average for the economy, resulting in a decline in relative prices.

The additional capital displaced unskilled workers more than it did skilled workers. Manufacturers added to the number of professional, managerial, and clerical workers. While the number of production workers employed fell at the rate of 1.6 percent between 1980 and 1986, the number of nonproduction workers increased slightly. "Production workers" refers to nonsupervisory workers employed in the plants, as opposed to nonplant offices. Thus, the proportion of office workers grew. The relative growth of the number of professional, managerial, and clerical workers in the eighties continues a long trend. Capital has been substituted more easily for unskilled factory workers than for other types of labor. In 1954 production workers made up 77 percent of the total number of persons employed in manufacturing, compared to 65 percent in 1985.[15]

However, the use of more capital and more office workers does not appear to explain a large part of the productivity gain in the eighties. Most of the improvement came simply from greater efficiency. Technological advances in production were one source. Another was the abandonment of old, relatively inefficient plants. A third may have been greater competitive pressure during the recession of 1981–82 and from the growth of imports. Under the gun of more intense competition, managers may have found ways to economize the use of labor. However, whatever greater productivity does for competitiveness, it hardly appears to be the remedy for a decline in manufacturing employment.

The fact that productivity growth has displaced labor may not dissuade policymakers from pursuing higher employment in manufacturing. They may hope to find a remedy for unemployment and for the shift of workers to low-paid service jobs in demand-promoting measures. If U.S. manufacturers succeeded in retaining a larger share of the U.S. market through market-sharing agreements with the Japanese, they would be able to produce more goods and thus possibly employ more workers.

Consider the possibilities. Judging from the regrets about the decline in manufacturing's share of total employment, one of the goals of an industrial policy would be to maintain this share. However, this would have been an unrealistic goal between 1980 and

1987, given the productivity growth. Output would have had to grow at the rate of 4.4 percent—29 percent faster than the actual 3.4 percent rate.[16] Even the more modest goal of maintaining employment at the same level would have been unrealistic. Output would have had to grow at the rate of 4.2 percent. The demand for manufactured goods was unlikely to grow at almost twice the growth rate for the other sectors combined.

Thus, better productivity, not competitive failure, explains the decline of employment in manufacturing. Better competitive performance was responsible for the decrease in the number of manufacturing workers. Not only is the case for an industrial policy based on a misreading of the cause of the decline, no policy would have succeeded in maintaining manufacturing's employment without sacrificing the gains in productivity.

While the gains benefited the entire population by reducing prices, those workers who became unemployed or accepted low-wage jobs suffered. As we have seen, it was production workers who were displaced, not professional or office workers. Moreover, for professional or office workers it makes little difference whether they work in manufacturing or in service industries. It is the displaced production workers who become unskilled service industry workers. In 1986 there were 1.3 million fewer production workers in manufacturing than in 1980—a drop of 6.4 percent.

Overall, despite the foreign competition and the shift into service industries, real hourly compensation in the economy as a whole rose by 3.7 percent between 1980 and 1987.[17] Compensation includes fringe benefits; the business sector excludes government, nonprofit enterprises, and households. Modest as it was, the increase in real compensation would have been even smaller without the rapid productivity growth in manufacturing and the resulting shift of workers into other industries.

THE PERFORMANCE OF INDIVIDUAL MANUFACTURING INDUSTRIES

If the president were to adopt an industrial policy, his objective would be to maintain or raise employment in manufacturing, more particularly in those industries where employment was falling. However, it would not make much sense to assist industries where employment fell because productivity was already growing rapidly. Since much of the drop in manufacturing as a whole has been due to productivity growth, we can expect to observe the same thing in most individual industries. It would hardly do to assist firms manufacturing, say, air conditioners if the drop in employment in that industry is due to greater efficiency.

If we eliminate such industries from the list of those to be assisted, what is left? A fall in employment will be due either to better efficiency or to a drop in output. A fall in output may be due to the loss of markets, as the advocates of an industrial policy suggest. If the fall in employment in the production of air conditioners was due to a loss of sales, then this industry would be a candidate for assistance.

However, the loss of sales need not be due to competition from abroad. Japanese manufacturers may not be capturing more and more of the market. The loss of sales may be due to the contraction of the market as a whole. Because households are well supplied with air conditioners, the market may have dried up. The administration should not undertake to assist declining industries that are in that position because demand has fallen off. Demand may have declined in various industries for different reasons. Steel may be displaced by aluminum or by plastics. To assist the industry with subsidies in that case would be inappropriate. Taxpayers would be paying manufacturers to compensate for the effects of reductions in the costs of producing other materials. Nor would tariff protection be appropriate, since it would not be imports that were the source of the decline in consumption.

Among the major industry groups, large drops in employment occurred in textiles; apparel; chemicals; stone, clay, and glass products; primary metals; fabricated metals; and nonelectrical machinery. In nearly all of these groups, productivity growth accounted for the major part of the loss of employment. Only in primary metal products was the loss of sales largely responsible.

The primary metals group, which includes steel, conforms most closely to the case envisaged by industrial policy proponents. However, even here an industrial policy that was designed to assist the industry in meeting foreign competition would be inappropriate. It was not foreign competition that was the main element in reducing output. The decline in domestic consumption was chiefly responsible, not the decline in exports or the rise of imports. The industrial planners could hardly compel users to desist from substituting plastic for steel and aluminum.

We sometimes hear the pro-industrial policy argument that shifting employment to high-tech industries, which employ skilled workers earning high wages, will raise average earnings. Japan again is cited as the model. MITI allegedly has subsidized those industries requiring highly-skilled workers. The period under review saw relatively rapid growth in the output of nonelectrical machinery, electrical machinery, instruments, and rubber and plastics, which are high-tech in comparison with those where output declined or did not grow, including primary metals; lumber and wood products; stone, clay, and glass products; fabricated metals; textile mills; and apparel. On the whole, manufacturing output shifted from low-tech to high-tech industries. Following the pro-industrial policy argument, this shift should have raised average earnings. We can observe in support of the argument that wages in the rapidly growing industries were higher than in the declining or slow-growth industries.

Average earnings in manufacturing did not improve greatly. Real hourly compensation increased by 3.2 percent over the entire period 1980–86.[18] Although output grew relatively in the high-tech industries, their high productivity growth offset the effect of the growth of output on average earnings. Employment did not shift to these industries. If the shifts had not occurred, earnings would have increased nearly as much.

COMPARISONS WITH PRODUCTIVITY GROWTH IN OTHER COUNTRIES

Those who worry about our competitiveness in world markets say that the United States has been lagging behind other countries in productivity growth. Thurow argues that to compete against Japan, U.S. manufacturing needs to accelerate its productivity growth. The call for higher productivity ignores its effect on employment. Nevertheless, the concern over lagging productivity has been so prevalent that it demands attention.

Thurow suggests that managers in this country are too taken up with short-term gains in sales and in profits to pay much attention to improvements in methods of production that will pay off only over a long period. He contrasts this attitude with that of Japanese managers, who are more patient. Thurow proposes that managers' total compensation be based on profits earned after they retire. They will receive bonuses after they retire that will reward their efforts to improve efficiency. Thurow also suggests that U.S. manufacturers imitate the Japanese by paying their workers partly with profit-sharing bonuses, which will enhance their incentive for efficiency. He also proposes that the administration select certain industries for assistance whose prospects are good. His only suggestion is ceramics.

Usually the United States is compared with Japan and West Germany in manufacturing productivity growth. In earlier periods, U.S. manufacturing did lag in productivity growth behind Japan and West Germany, as well as other countries. However, in the eighties U.S. manufacturing outstripped West Germany and the lag behind Japan was cut. Between 1980 and 1987 productivity per hour in U.S. manufacturing rose at the rate of 3.8 percent compared to 2.8 percent for West Germany and 4.7 percent for Japan. Moreover, it was faster than the growth in Canada, France, Denmark, Norway, and Sweden. U.S. growth was slower than the growth in Italy and the UK. Productivity growth in U.S. manufacturing was better than the average for the West.[19]

Since the doomsayers' primary concern has been with markets, we should also see how well the United States has been performing in the international output growth race. U.S. manufacturing has not done badly. The 3.4 percent rate of growth between 1980 and 1987 far exceeded the 0.9 percent rate of growth in West Germany. The U.S. growth rate also was much higher than those of other OECD countries, excluding Japan. The range for these countries was −0.1 to 1.9 percent. On the other hand, Japan's manufacturing output grew at the much higher rate of 5.6 percent.[20]

It is interesting to observe that U.S. manufacturing's success in selling did not rely on the devaluation of the dollar, which only began late in 1985. Thus, between 1980 and 1985 the rate of growth of output for the United States was the same as for 1980–87: 3.4 percent. The Japanese rate was higher before the dollar came down than after. Over the period 1980–85, Japan's output grew at the rate of 7.3 percent. The high dollar appears to have benefited Japan especially. On the other hand, Germany's output growth rate was low in this period: 0.6 percent.[21] On the whole, U.S. manufacturing did relatively well despite the high dollar.

These numbers suggest that the rise in productivity in U.S. manufacturing made it competitive with manufacturing in other countries. However, we should not forget that other factors contributed to the growth of U.S. manufacturing output, including the slow rate of growth of wages. Real average hourly compensation in manufacturing in the United States rose much less than in other OECD countries. United States earnings rose at the average annual rate of 0.2 percent between 1980 and 1987. The rates for Japan and Germany were 2.1 percent and 2.4 percent, respectively. In other OECD countries the range was from 0.5 percent to 2.2 percent.[22]

FOREIGN COMPETITION

Reading the news, we keep seeing reports of the fall of exports and the rise of imports. But exports are not the total market, and domestic output can expand despite import growth. U.S. manufacturing output may grow even if exports drop and imports take a bigger share of the total domestic market. With attention focused on exports and imports, we may get a distorted picture of the state of manufacturing. We also read that our share of the world market in many products has fallen. Although the popular measure of competitive strength has been the share of the world market, it is invalid. A declining U.S. share is inevitable inasmuch as it was huge in the early postwar period before Japan and Western Europe had had a chance to recover from the war. We can also expect it to decline because the growth of output in developing countries will be more rapid. Moreover, the world market may be growing rapidly enough to permit U.S. sales to increase, despite a fall in the American share of total sales.

Foreign competition tended to reduce employment in manufacturing because it reduced U.S. exports and raised U.S. imports. Nevertheless, as we have seen, total output increased. A balanced picture requires that we look at the growth of domestic consumption as well as at the growth of imports and exports. Even if we export fewer aircraft than last year and imports of Europe's Airbus aircraft take a larger share of the U.S. airlines' purchases, Boeing's output may still grow. And Boeing's output may still grow even if its share of the world market is smaller. The omitted critical element is how many more aircraft the domestic airlines are purchasing. If initially exports and imports are small relative to the total domestic output, then if the domestic market grows Boeing can still do very well. The output of U.S. manufacturing industries grew in the eighties because domestic consumption did. The increase in domestic consumption was greater than the sum of the decline in exports and the increase in imports.

The domestic consumption of manufactured products grew at a sufficiently rapid rate to more than offset the effects of the decline in exports and the growth of imports. The growth of domestic consumption, which was more than twice the sum of the decline in exports and the growth of imports, permitted manufacturing output to grow. Obviously, foreign competitors gained a larger share of the U.S. and world markets. But U.S. manufacturing output did not shrink.

U.S. manufacturing output, as we have seen, continues to climb at a rate that exceeds that of other developed countries. The only exception is Japan. Employment has fallen in U.S. manufacturing, but this has been due to productivity advances, not to weaker competitive strength. Indeed, better competitive performance will be associated with declining employment, not with increasing employment.

The domestic consumption of nonelectrical machinery products has grown at a phenomenal rate. Domestic consumption has been responsible for virtually all of the increase in the output of this group. Moreover, the group increased its competitive strength according to the popular measure mentioned earlier. The growth of exports has far exceeded the growth of imports, Japan notwithstanding.

The trade record for electrical machinery has not been as good as for nonelectrical machinery. Imports have grown much faster than exports. However, the growth of domestic consumption has been sufficiently rapid to permit a large increase in the output of the industry. The same thing can be said about the instruments, paper products, and rubber and plastics industries.

The decline in output of the primary metals group has attracted a lot of attention. But foreign competition is not the chief cause, as is commonly believed. The group's troubles spring mainly from the fall in domestic consumption. The fall in domestic consumption has contributed twice as much as the changes in exports and imports to the decline in output. Moreover, imports contributed very little to the fall in output. A protectionist policy would have done little to maintain employment in this group.

Transport equipment, including motor vehicles, has had to withstand strong foreign competition. Imports have grown sharply and exports have fallen. On the whole, however, output has held its own. The growth in domestic consumption has offset the drop in exports and the growth of imports.

CONCLUSION

An industrial policy is unlikely to raise the general standard of living. It will protect some industries that have the necessary clout. Some public funds will probably go into new or existing plants in depressed areas. Labor-management-government committees may try to regulate competition in steel, apparel, textiles, and other depressed industries. The policy will not revive these industries and it may harm their performance. Foreign competitive pressures have forced firms even in these industries to improve their efficiency. Limiting the pressures by reducing import quotas is unlikely to force firms to cut costs. A review of the behavior of the auto industry by Robert Crandall of the Brookings Institution suggests that the VRA has eased up the pressure on the firms there—that productivity would have improved more rapidly in an open competitive market.

American manufacturing has performed well in the eighties. Growing imports and the loss of exports probably gave firms the impetus to raise their productivity. The recession added to the pressure. The rise in productivity has been chiefly responsible for the fall in employment in manufacturing. On the whole, however, the gain in productivity cannot be viewed as anything but beneficial. The losses suffered by some workers are unfortunate. These losses are the inevitable consequence of change. Unemployment insurance and social security benefits limit the losses, and these may be improved. An industrial policy would seek to prevent workers from being hurt by economic change by limiting competition. Moreover, it is misdirected. The losses of income by former manufacturing workers has not resulted from excessive foreign competition but from rapid productivity growth. The implementation of an industrial policy program will inhibit economic growth and slow down the rise in the standard of living for the population as a whole.

7
STATE AND LOCAL GOVERNMENT SERVICES

While our major concern is the federal government, we should not neglect the state and local governments. All governments draw revenues from the same pool. The federal government taxes personal incomes, and most state and some city governments do as well. So far the federal government has not trespassed on the state and local governments' turf by imposing a general sales tax, but it may soon break its implicit word by enacting a value-added tax, which would be similar to a sales tax. Even now state governments are squeezed when the federal government increase its tax rates. It was the growth of the federal tax burden that broke the taxpayers' backs, bringing on the tax revolt at the state and local level initiated in California in the late seventies by Howard Jarvis.

Those who live and raise families in major cities would easily agree that state and local government services have deteriorated. By state and local government services, I mean those that are primarily the responsibility of these governments. I refer to education, fire protection, highways, police protection, and sanitation. The federal government also spends money on these services, but the state and local governments have the primary responsibility. Therefore, for convenience, I will refer to these as the state and local government services. Those of us who remember the fifties can see that the city streets are in much worse condition than they were then. New Yorkers deny afflictions by describing them as pleasures. Just as they have boasted about the high quality of subway graffiti art, they pride themselves on having the nation's biggest potholes. Bridges had to collapse before policymakers initiated a campaign of restoration, and the highways are in a sad state. It is easier to put off maintenance expenditures than to raise taxes. Unless a mayor is in office for a long time, the consequences of the neglect will be visited only on his or her successors. Crime rates have increased. Only the brave walk on some city streets at night. In 1986 the number of crimes committed per capita of population was six and one-half times as large as in 1950.[1] Jails now are so over-crowded that small thefts are not enough to get into one. In 1986 the number of prisoners per capita of population was almost double that of 1950.[2] Sanitation services also have deteriorated. Getting rid of waste grows more difficult and costly as the quantities multiply and disposal sites become scarcer. Moreover, the flow of the poor from the rural areas into the big cities in the postwar period has increased the need for health services, hospitals, public aid, housing, social services, and police protection.

The explanation is not simple. No single cause can be blamed for the decline of the quality of state and local services. Costs have risen greatly, taxpayers prefer to spend their money for other things, and governments are spending more money on transfer payments, including social security benefits, unemployment ben-efits, and welfare. Consider the costs of the services first. Teachers, police officers, firemen, and sanitation workers may be paid lower wages than equally-skilled workers in other occupations. Whether or not they are is uncertain. What is clear is that wages paid by state and local governments have risen at about the same rate as the general wage level. Wages, of course, are the major cost by far of the state and local services. We also know that productivity growth in government services, as in other services, has been much slower than in manufacturing. The number of labor hours required to perform a particular government service, such as teaching a child the alphabet or removing a ton of garbage, has fallen less than the number of hours required to manufacture a car. As a result, the costs of teaching children and of removing garbage have risen rel-ative to the cost of manufacturing cars. In 1950 for the purchase price of an average car one could buy teaching the alphabet to perhaps 1,000 children. Now, the purchase price of a car could only buy teaching, say, 250 children the alphabet. These figures are only illustrative, but if they were true then teaching would have become four times as expensive in units of cars as in 1950.

Advances in science and in technical knowledge more generally have paid off in greater productivity throughout the economy, and we also have a more skilled labor force thanks to more workers having graduated from high school or college than in 1950. As a result, the general standard of living has risen: In constant dollars the GNP per capita nearly doubled between 1950 and 1986.

However, productivity growth has been slow wherever personal service is supplied, as in restaurants. Sure, restaurants now have automatic dishwashers, food processors, and microwave ovens. But waiting on tables, preparing food, cooking, and cleaning up remain labor intensive. Some savings have been achieved, but not much. Fast-food restaurants may appear to have gained considerably in productivity. But much of the gain is only apparent, since the reductions in labor hours have been at the cost of quality, at least to some extent. Barber shops, laundries and cleaners, shoe repair, auto repair, and hotels also have seen slow productivity growth. The opportunities for productivity advances are greater in manufacturing than in the service sector because the highly routinized procedures of manufacturing operations lend themselves more to being speeded up and to mechanization than does service work.

Educational, police, fire protection, and sanitation services resemble the services of the private sector in offering limited scope for speed up and for mechanization. Teaching long division takes as much time as it ever did. Apparent economies may be achieved in schools by increasing class size. The savings are only apparent because the quality of education suffers. In large classes elementary and high school students receive less individual attention. It is hard to arrest a perpetrator quickly. Cities may save by taking police officers off the beat and putting them into cars. But removed from neighborhoods, they lose knowledge of the residents, and the quality of enforcement suffers. Apparent gains in productivity may only reflect quality deterioration.

The Bureau of Economic Analysis of the Department of Commerce includes changes in quality in its estimates of the growth of output. It does not simply measure the output of the auto industry by counting the number of cars produced. It allows for changes in the size and weight and for improvements in transmissions, batteries, engines, brakes, and other components. These estimates are difficult, especially for services. The estimates of productivity, which is output per unit of labor plus other inputs, may be based on exaggerated estimates of the growth of the output of services because they understate quality deterioration. The estimates may not recognize the worsening of the quality of education resulting from the decline in teachers' skills, increases in class size, and the deterioration of physical facilities.

In any case, the gains in productivity in the service industries, including those in the public sector, have been far less than in manufacturing. As a result, the prices of manufactured goods rose much less than those of services generally and of state and local services in particular. Because productivity advanced more rapidly in the manufacture of durable goods, such as cars, air conditioners, TV sets, and toasters, prices of such goods rose less than those of any other category. Between 1950 and 1986 the prices of durable manufactured goods rose at the average annual rate of 2.4 percent and those of nondurable manufactured goods at the rate of 3.5 percent.[3] The prices of services in the private sector rose at the average annual rate of 4.7 percent. Over the same period, the rate of increase of the costs of state and local government services was 5.4 percent. Because of the greater difficulty of measuring quality changes in services, the prices of services probably rose more than these estimates indicate. Accepting at face value these estimates of price increases, the price increase for government services was much greater than for manufactured goods. They rose even in relation to the prices of services provided by the private sector.

The effect of these increases in costs is to reduce the quantity and quality of the services purchased. Taxpayers will resist increases in tax rates and the imposition of new taxes to pay the higher costs of maintaining the services at the same level.

Of course, people individually and collectively through their governments do not respond only to prices when they make purchases. Thus, even though prices of privately supplied services went up much more than the prices of nondurable goods, the consumption of such services grew much more rapidly. The consumption of privately supplied services increased at the average annual rate of 3.7 percent compared to 2.5 percent for nondurable goods. These services include the use of residential housing. One reason for the boom in privately supplied services was that more women were working outside the home. The cooking, which in 1970 they had done themselves (which was not counted as part of consumption), in 1986 they purchased from restaurants. Moreover, as their incomes grew, people went to the movies more often, travelled more, and paid more visits to doctors. In addition, newly-married couples moved to the suburbs where their cottages gave them more space than inner-city apartments did.

Durable goods became much cheaper relative to other goods and services. Many new items became popular, including TV sets, air conditioners, home freezers, high fidelity audio equipment, and more recently video cassette recorders, microwave ovens, food processors, and microcomputers. Established products, including cars and refrigerators, were improved and their relative prices came down. The consumption of durables also grows more than proportionally with income, and over this period constant-dollar disposable personal income per capita more than doubled.[4] Disposable income is income after taxes. Thus, the quantity of durable goods consumed grew at the rate of 4.4 percent compared to an average annual rate of growth of 3.1 percent for real GNP. Expressed another way, the quantity of durable goods consumed grew nearly five times over the period, while GNP tripled.

Before taking up the growth in the quantity of state and local services purchased, we should say something about the growth of transfer payments and of defense expenditures. Between 1950 and 1986 transfer payments by governments, including social security payments, benefits to retired government workers, unemployment insurance benefits, and welfare payments, grew enormously. The elderly, who gained political power as their numbers grew, won higher social security benefits. In the early seventies Congress voted to grant pensioners a cost-of-living allowance. Benefits were to keep pace with the consumer price index. Welfare payments also grew as the proportion of the poor receiving benefits increased. The costs were paid for by increases in social security taxes, increases in revenue resulting from inflation and from the growth of total income, and by increases in tax rates by state and local governments.

Real transfer payments increased at the high rate of 4.9 percent.[5] Expressed differently, over the period in question, these expenditures in constant dollars grew six times, or twice as much as the GNP.

On the other hand, defense expenditures in constant dollars have grown very slowly. The average annual rate of increase over the period was only 0.8 percent.[6] This slow rate of growth released resources for other purposes.

Let us first review the numbers relating to services largely provided by state and local governments. The federal government has contributed money to supporting these services, but, as I said earlier, for convenience I refer to them as state and local services. The measures of growth include federal expenditures. The annual rates of growth of state and local services were higher than the rate of growth of real GNP and about the same as the rate of growth of private services. Real expenditures on education grew at the rate of 3.8 percent, fire protection services at 3.4 percent, and sanitation services at 3.7 percent. Expenditures for health services and hospitals grew at the rate of 4.6 percent. The rate for highways was much less—2.2 percent. The rates for police protection and for public welfare were much higher. Constant-dollar expenditures for police protection grew at the rate of 4.6 percent and public welfare expenditures at the rate of 4.9 percent.[7]

However, as we have seen, crime rates have risen, jails are overcrowded, and the sanitation services appear to have deteriorated. One explanation for the inconsistency between the measures of the growth of expenditures and the apparent decline in the quality of the services is that with the growth of population and with its increased urbanization, expenditures must increase merely to maintain the same level of quality.

The inconsistency between the numbers describing the growth of state and local services, apart from education and roads, and the apparent quality of the services may be due to poor measures. Evaluating the quality of services is very difficult. The measures therefore may exaggerate the growth of the real quantity, corrected for quality, of the services provided.

Finally, constant-dollar expenditures for services may have increased, but the problems with which the state and local governments have to cope have also increased. Many crimes are drug related, and the drug problem has gotten much worse since 1950. A large part of the work of police relates to traffic control. Problems of traffic congestion have increased enormously with the car population.

The schools have a greater task than in the past. With many more married women working outside the home, the care of children has deteriorated. As a result, education at the elementary and secondary levels has suffered. It may not be possible even with much larger expenditures to offset the effect of the reduction in the number of hours mothers are at home.

In addition, as technology advances, workers need more skills. The labor force has become better educated over the years, and skills have improved as a result. The proportion of workers in professional and skilled clerical jobs has grown. The proportion in unskilled factory jobs has fallen. However, a large part of the population remains unskilled. In the 25-to-34-year age group, in 1986 as many as 13 percent had not completed four years of high school.[8] Many of these dropouts never acquire a high level of skill, and many of them suffer long periods of unemployment. As production processes become more automated and computers take over more clerical work, the uneducated will have greater difficulty finding employment.

THE NEED FOR MORE REVENUE

One conclusion that has widespread support is that more resources should be devoted to education. There is general agreement that school boards have to raise the quality of teaching and that to attract better teachers, they need to be paid more. In addition, since children need to learn more now than they did previously to gain entry into skilled occupations, the school day should be lengthened and the number of school days per year should be increased. The length of the school year has not risen over many decades, despite the increase in the amount to be learned and in the demand for higher skills. The traditional length is a hangover from our rural past, and in the last decade of the twentieth century we should reevaluate the additional learning that can be gained with extra days in school. Other countries have lengthened their school years. We should do the same. For the same reason, children will benefit from additional hours in school each day. A longer school day also will relieve the problems of child care for two-earner families. The schools have to take over more of the task of raising children. However, to require classroom teachers to undertake more work, they will have to be paid more, over and above an increase intended to attract better teachers.

Nor is there much disagreement about the need for more funds for streets, roads, and bridges. The neglect of maintenance has resulted in widespread, severe deterioration. Continued neglect because of other competing demands for funds risks increasingly hazardous conditions.

The cities and states need more funds for the police and for the administration of justice generally. Although the resources devoted to these purposes have grown considerably over the years, expenditures remain inadequate. Crime becomes an increasingly urgent problem, and the need for larger police forces for other purposes has also become more pressing.

There is little room for cutting expenditures by state and local governments. Sanitation and sewage problems are not becoming easier. Cities are having trouble meeting the national environmental standards. Social service problems are becoming worse, and more funds will have to be spent on public aid. The number of homeless has grown enormously in the last few years, and the cities have the problem of sheltering them.

The state and local governments need more funds. They are in a poor position to raise taxes. The tax revolt (about which Chapter 8 says more) continues. A sure road to defeat for a politician is to propose a larger burden for taxpayers. In addition, one way in which the states and cities compete for taxpaying companies and residents is by promising lower tax rates.

The federal government makes substantial contributions to state and local governments. In 1985 they added up to $106 billion, or 15 percent of the total state and local government revenues.[9] Most of the assistance was allocated to welfare assistance, highways, and education. The federal assistance grew enormously between 1970 and 1980—by 73 percent in constant dollars. However, this assistance was one of the victims of the Reagan drive to cut nondefense expenditures. It is estimated that in 1988 the assistance was 16 percent less than in 1980.[10]

The federal government should increase its assistance to the state and local governments. The assistance immediately should be raised back to the level of 1980 in constant dollars. The additional money should be spent on improving education, where the need is most urgent and where there is no problem of specifying how it should be spent. The highest priority should be given to raising teachers' salaries. The more difficult tasks of lengthening school days and years will take more time to accomplish. If funds remain after raising teachers' salaries, then the next highest priority is the administration of justice. Congress has made funds available recently for highway and bridge maintenance, so this is less urgent. Looking further ahead, the federal government should prepare to make more funds available for state and local government services.

8

THE DEFICIT AND TAXES

The big tax cut enacted in 1981 together with a generous defense purse opened up a huge gap between revenues and expenditures, which Reagan left to his successor to close. The Bush administration will find it hard to fob off the task to the next one.

The administration faces immediate pressures from foreign central banks and governments to bring the deficit down. The large speculative purchases and sales of the dollar impose external constraints on the administration's fiscal policy. The Carter administration could ignore foreign governments in reaching fiscal policy decisions. The dollar fluctuated, but until the eighties it did not go through wild gyrations. In recent years, the value of the dollar in foreign exchange markets has depended on speculators' expectations of the real interest rate in the United States relative to real interest rates elsewhere. If speculators, including necessarily multinationals, which hold large cash balances in different currencies, expect the real interest rate in the United States to rise, they will buy dollars and thus push up its value. If they expect it to fall, they will sell and push down its value.

The administration wants to avoid instability. A high dollar hurts exporters, and a falling dollar risks inflation in the present period when some types of labor are in short supply and domestic demand continues to grow. The administration depends on the cooperation of foreign central banks to prevent a rapid rise or fall in the dollar. Until very recently, the Bank of Japan, the Bundesbank, and other central banks desperately propped up the dollar by pouring money into U.S. Treasury bills, and their help may be needed again. Buying dollars is a risky business, for when it falls the buyer suffers losses in yen, marks, pounds, or other currencies. The foreign central banks already have lost a great deal of money on past dollar accumulations, and they may refuse to take another beating.

Since they believe that the political cowardice in dealing with the deficit is responsible for the decline in the dollar (as well as for its earlier rise), they may be mulish in their bargaining. At not very convivial meetings, the foreign central bankers regularly have demanded that the United States cut its deficit, and regularly Treasury Secretary James Baker said that it would. If the foreign central bankers carry through with their threat and withdraw their support, the Fed may have to risk a recession by raising the interest rate. What is more, bankers, economists, and others in this country agree with the Bundesbank and the Bank of Japan.

Chapter 3 argued that the federal deficit was neither the sole nor the most important source of the high interest rate and the high dollar when it was high. It also argued that the deficit was not responsible for its fall. What is more, currently the real interest rate in this country is not high in comparison with the West German and Japanese real interest rates. If it does rise, it will be because the Fed and investors generally fear inflation. A rise will have little to do with the deficit.

Nevertheless, the Bush administration is unlikely to keep tax rates down and allow expenditures to keep mounting. Thus we have to know how the deficit may be closed. To help to understand how the deficit came to be, we will review the history of Reagan's tax cut. We will see that the cut was a vote-getting effort. There was nothing inevitable about it.

The federal government raises taxes to pay for services and to transfer income between various groups in the population. The primary service provided by the federal government is defense against external enemies. Defense therefore takes up over 30 percent of the total budget. The major part of total outlays consists of shifts of income. The second largest item in the budget is social security. Most of the payments under this heading are to old age pensioners; money is shifted from the current working population to the retired. Welfare and other poverty assistance programs and farm support programs also are transfers of income from taxpayers as a whole to special groups. Other expenditures are for the administration of justice and the operation of such agencies as the post office, the parks services, the Environmental Protection Agency, and for general government. Together, the federal outlays make up 23 percent of the GNP.[1]

The present chapter discusses tax rates and the pressure for reductions. Reagan's dubious, great achievement was to reduce tax rates. Despite this reduction, the share of the GNP spent on government has grown. The proper way to discuss fiscal policy is to review tax receipts in conjunction with expenditures. But it is difficult to talk about both taxes and expenditures simultaneously. So we begin with taxes.

HOW THE TAX CUT CAME ABOUT

It was obvious that the tax cut enacted in 1981 plus the planned jump in defense expenditures would break the budget. For the moment, we shall look only at the tax cuts. An economic theory—the supply-side theory—permitted Reagan to keep his respectability with journalists, TV talk show participants, and others who influence voters. Candidates' arguments may not grab much attention, but votes may be swung by broadcasters' snide remarks. The press can destroy a candidate, as Gary Hart and Joseph Biden learned. Reagan was able to get away with making his extravagant promise by propounding the supply-side theory. This theory argued that the then high income tax rates destroyed investors' and workers' incentives. A cut in these rates would stimulate growth in the GNP and therefore in the tax revenues. No deficit would result. Doubts about its validity did not prevent the theory from shielding him against the correct accusation of reckless opportunism. The issue of the theory's validity dominated the debate, not the issue of opportunism. Journalists could not destroy Reagan with the accusation of dishonest electioneering.

At the same time, Reagan sounded the bugle for weapons. He accused Carter of allowing our defenses to deteriorate while the Soviets frenetically built up their forces.

The money was to come from the growth in GNP stimulated by the tax cut and from eliminating government waste. No previous candidate had flayed government waste as much. However, a clean up was not enough. Taxes could not be lowered and defense expenditures raised as much as Reagan wanted without incurring a large deficit. However, Reagan did not wake up suddenly one morning an extreme deficit-loving Keynesian. Retaining his credentials as a staunch fiscal conservative, he condemned Carter's deficits. Advancing the supply-side theory was a great trick. Reagan gained an enormous advantage over his rivals for the nomination and over Carter in the 1980 election campaign. He could cheerfully advocate lower taxes and higher expenditures. The other Republican candidates for the nomination could not offer the same theory once Reagan advanced it, to say nothing of Carter.

The tax appeal is always powerful, but it was especially so at that time. Ordinary working couples, not only high-salaried yuppie executives, were having much of their hard-earned, modest incomes deducted at the source for taxes. Even unskilled factory workers, whose Saturday night treat was a dinner at McDonald's before their bowling game, never saw a large part of their incomes. Working wives suffered most. Their small wages were added to their husbands' and therefore taxed at a high rate. By 1980, 60 percent of married women between the ages of 25 and 44 held jobs, and with the average husband earning $20,000 and the average wife earning $10,000, many couples were in a high tax bracket. Suppose the couple had two children. Their federal marginal income tax rate—the rate paid on the last dollar earned—was 30 percent. Including social security taxes, it was 36 percent. Adding state income taxes, the total easily came to 39 percent after the federal deduction. There were also the transportation and child-care costs. Many supermarket cashiers must have wondered whether the daily long hours standing on their feet and being harassed by customers, followed by household chores, were worth the after-tax earnings. No wonder 40 percent of married women stayed home. Magazine articles glamorize well-dressed, well-coiffed lawyers carrying briefcases who prefer answering interrogatories to house cleaning, not the more numerous waitresses. Reagan did not promise a bed of roses, but he offered more than the other candidates.

By 1980, taxpayers were in revolt. After California adopted Howard Jarvis's Proposition 13 reducing property taxes, the revolt caught fire. In 1977 Congressman Jack Kemp and Senator William

Roth introduced a bill to cut personal income taxes across all brackets uniformly by 10 percent each year for three successive years.

Reagan's primary campaign needed luster after Bush's strong showing, and government inefficiency was too old a whipping horse. Harping on government extravagance also may have risked frightening millions of social security and food stamp beneficiaries.

But featuring the Kemp-Roth tax cut and making it the centerpiece of his campaign risked a barrage of ridicule. Kemp and his supporters, including Congressman David Stockman and economist Arthur Laffer, supplied the needed simple theory. Media pundits had to be persuaded that Reagan was not simply bribing voters with an impossible handout. The theory persuasively argued that the heavy tax burden made investors averse to risks and workers reluctant to work long, hard hours; a large tax cut would invigorate the economy.

In its general form and without any numbers attached to it, there was nothing wrong with the argument. Everyone could easily agree that a reduction in the gain from investment or work reduced incentives. By itself, this soporific, familiar case might have won general agreement. But to say that the resulting gain in GNP would eliminate the deficit implied a very powerful, large effect on incentives. No one really knew what the effect would be, and it was unlikely to be sufficient to prevent a deficit.

Nevertheless, the proponents made this claim. Assuring the public that no deficit would result, Kemp parted company with most economists by insisting that the government would lose no revenue. The 30 percent tax cut would spur so much more output that total revenue would at least remain the same or even grow.

The case consisted of nothing more than assertions. Laffer drew what became known as the Laffer Curve relating tax revenue to the tax rate. Starting with a zero rate and no revenue, the revenue went up as the rate rose. As the rate rose further beyond some undefined point, the revenue began to fall. Revenue reached zero again when the rate reached 100 percent. The Laffer Curve enshrined the great discovery that the tax rate yielding the highest revenue was somewhere between 0 and 100 percent. Laffer drew a symmetrical curve that reached its peak in the middle, suggesting that the maximum revenue rate was 50 percent. Laffer did not say that this was the magic rate. The curve simply happened to reach its peak in the middle. Of course, he did not intend this interpretation, for it would have implied raising the rate for most taxpayers. To make his case, Laffer had to show that the current tax rates were in the declining range where revenues fell as the rates rose and that a 30 percent cut in rates would move them closer to the maximum revenue point.

Even this argument would not have been adequate. For the revenues to remain the same, a 30 percent reduction of tax rates would have had to induce a 40 percent rise in incomes. Unless incomes increased by this amount, the lower rates were bound to produce less revenue.

Laffer pointed to Kennedy's tax cut in 1964. But the Kennedy cut, which was much smaller than the one proposed, had occurred in a noninflationary, depressed economy. In sum, it did not establish that taxpayers would respond to a 30 percent cut by earning at least 40 percent more.

Indeed, ordinary workers could not earn higher wages by working harder, and they could not work much longer hours. A 40 percent increase would bring weekly hours up to the mid–50s! More women would find jobs, and some part-timers would begin to work full-time. But their contributions would not make up the needed difference.

Although maintaining total revenues at the same level would require much more labor effort and hours, Kemp and company ignored labor. Instead, they emphasized the incentives of entrepreneurs. Entrepreneurial risk-taking and capital are important, but entrepreneurs could not be counted on to do the whole job. In any case, the supply-siders were vague. Presumably, the entrepreneurs were the executives and proprietors of businesses. But how inefficient was business, and how quickly could the inefficiency be reduced by the required amount? Would companies that were afraid to risk capital in developing new technologies and products be suddenly willing to mount a major effort?

If the tax cut were to raise output, then the effect would show up in estimates of that part of the total growth of output due to advances in knowledge and improvements in efficiency. If we look at how much these sources of growth have contributed in the past, we can see that Kemp and company were offering a fantasy. According to Edward Denison, between 1929 and 1982 total output grew at an average annual rate of 2.92 percent. Of this total, 1.9 percentage points were due to increases in the number of labor hours, improvements in skills, and increases in the quantity of capital. This left 1.02 percentage points to other causes. Denison estimated that greater knowledge and improvements in efficiency contributed 0.66 percentage points. If the tax cut raised productivity growth, then this part of the total growth in output would be raised. Between 1948 and 1973 more knowledge and efficiency added 1.09 percentage points to the growth rate of the economy. Between 1973 and 1982 a slowdown took place and these sources contributed nothing to the growth of the economy.[2]

Suppose the tax cut was very effective in boosting output, as the supply-siders predicted. How much would a large improvement in efficiency add to the growth of total output? Judging from the past record, adding 1 percentage point to the growth rate of output would be very good. But such a magnificent performance would not be good enough. The budget would remain in deficit for many years. We can reasonably assume that without the tax cut both tax revenues and expenditures would continue to grow at the same rate as GNP. The tax cut would have to add 40 percent to GNP to eliminate the deficit. If it added 1 percentage point to the GNP growth rate, then it would take 34 years for the budget to come back into balance.

Conceivably, lower tax rates would do the trick over a long period, but in the meantime the deficits would be large. The tax cutters said that there would be no deficits, not that over a long period newly-released energies would bring the budget back into balance.

These obvious problems for the supply-side theory received no attention. The supporters of Kemp-Roth preferred to talk vaguely about enterprise and incentives. Relying on these slogans, they were not compelled to get down to the details of how much additional income could be expected.

Thus, in reality Reagan's platform implied much larger deficits. The economic theory gave the platform legitimacy by permitting Reagan to deny this implication, especially since the critics did not examine the numbers carefully enough to be completely persuasive. Even Bush's characterization of the case for the tax cut as "voodoo economics" did not show that a large deficit would result. Perhaps because he did not examine the tax cut in detail, his sarcasm was not repeated widely enough to hurt Reagan substantially.

Because the supply-siders denied that the tax cut would produce the anathema—a deficit—they did not have to consider its consequences for inflation and monetary policy. The chief economic problem at the time was inflation. A voter who was worried about skyrocketing prices might have been frightened rather than comforted by the promise of a tax cut. In 1979 prices were rising at a rate of over 11 percent; the next year the inflation rate was over 13 percent. Even before Paul Volcker became chairman in 1979, the Fed had been trying to slow down the pace of inflation. Volcker was unlikely to greet the prospect of a deficit joyfully, since it would complicate the Fed's task. A huge increase in the Treasury's bond issues to finance the larger deficit while the Fed was tightening the money supply would push the interest rate way up. Any business that wanted to buy new machinery might find the cost of financing it prohibitive. Kemp and company did not examine these effects of their proposed tax cut.

What about Reagan's other advisers? Surely, some of the prominent conservative economists such as George Shultz, Alan Greenspan, and the late Arthur Burns were shocked by the proposal. They would not have supported a politically motivated, dishonest platform certain to produce a large deficit. Shultz, Greenspan, and Burns must have recognized the fanciful nature of the forecasts of a balanced budget. Yet, whatever protests they may have expressed privately to Reagan, they remained publicly silent. Public criticism would risk being on the outs with the coming administration. Desperate for a winning platform, Reagan may have decided to ignore any cautions expressed by the nonradical right.

Apparently, some advisers favored a deficit, despite their acceptance of antideficit economic arguments. Pessimistic about Congress's profligacy, they saw a huge deficit as a device to use to force Congress to mend its ways. During the seventies expenditures for AFDC, social security, and other social programs had risen rapidly, as the growth of GNP and inflation fed federal revenues and defense expenditures dropped with the end of the Vietnam War. To allow tax revenues to continue to grow with GNP would only invite more congressional extravagance.

Reagan was elected, Congress passed the Economic Recovery

Tax Act, and the first installment of the tax cut came in the second half of 1981. The original Kemp-Roth bill had called for three cuts each of 10 percent in the personal income tax rate in three years. The act reduced the first cut to 5 percent—the total cut adding up to 25 percent.

Once the party started, Congress was even more eager than the president to cut the top tax rate and it went beyond Kemp-Roth. Congress joined the general exuberance; the members did not want to suffer voters' hostility and allow Reagan to bask in glory alone. They would give the high taxpayers, who happened also to be their chief campaign contributors, the benefit of a handout. The top rate of 70 percent was cut immediately to 50 percent; Congress did not want to spread out the reduction for the wealthy over three years.

Before treating the consequences of the act, we look at the other major tax legislation passed during the Reagan presidency—the Tax Reform Act of 1986. This legislation, which fully came into force in 1988, was intended to simplify the tax system without reducing revenues. It doubled the personal exemptions and increased the standard deduction, removing 4.8 million poor people from the tax rolls. The new schedule has four rates: 15, 28, 33, and 38 percent. The 33 percent rate is the result of phasing out the lowest tax rate and personal tax exemptions for high-income taxpayers. Those in the highest bracket now have a smaller incentive to invest in tax shelters and to evade taxes by padding expenses. Realized capital gains are taxed as ordinary income except for those on assets transferred by gift or at death. Deductions for state and local sales taxes and interest payments on consumer loans were removed. The deduction for contributions to individual retirement accounts by those already enrolled in private pension plans were restricted to only married taxpayers with incomes below $50,000 and to single taxpayers with incomes below $35,000.

The Tax Reform Act also reduced the corporate tax rate from 46 percent to 34 percent. However, it increased corporate taxes by eliminating the investment credit, reducing depreciation allowances for structures, and eliminating loopholes. Joseph Pechman estimates that the act raised corporate tax liabilities overall by about 20 percent.[3]

The new personal income tax rates do not climb with income as steeply as under the old law. Above a taxable income of $71,900

Table 8.1
Federal Receipts, Outlays, and Deficits in
Fiscal Years 1980-1987
(in billions of dollars)

	Receipts	Outlays	Deficits
1980	517.1	590.9	73.8
1981	599.3	678.2	78.9
1982	617.8	745.7	127.9
1983	600.6	808.3	207.8
1984	666.5	851.8	185.3
1985	734.1	946.3	212.3
1986	769.1	990.3	221.2
1987	854.1	1,004.6	150.4
1988	909.2	1,055.9	146.7

Source: Economic Report of the President 1988, p. 337.

it stops climbing for a married couple with two children. Never-theless, Democrats supported the reform. Indeed, the act was more Senator Bill Bradley's child than the administration's. It was not Bradley's intention to ease the tax burden of the rich. He saw that Congress had eroded the progressivity of the nominal tax schedule by creating tax shelters to promote the drilling of oil wells, the construction of low-cost housing, the financing of state and municipal governments, and other worthy enterprises. The rich escaped taxation on income from investments in sheltered limited partnerships.

THE TAX CUT AND THE DEFICIT

Fiscal year 1982 (October 1, 1981 to September 31, 1982), saw the deficit climb from $78.9 billion to $127.9 billion (Table 8.1). Between 1983 and 1986 the increase exceeded $200 billion per year, except in 1984 when it was $185.3 billion. In 1987 it was $150.0 billion and in 1988, $146.7 billion.

The tax cut and the rise in defense expenditures, which is discussed in Chapter 9, accounted for nearly all of the deficit.

As we shall see later, it is virtually impossible to eliminate the

Table 8.2
Percentages of Federal Receipts
by Major Category, 1987

Individual income taxes	46.0
Corporation income taxes	9.8
Social insurance taxes	35.3
Other receipts*	8.7
Total	100.0

Source: Economic Report of the President 1988, p. 339.
*Excise taxes, estate and gift taxes, customs duties, earnings of Federal Reserve system, other.

deficit by cutting expenditures. There is little room for further cuts in nondefense expenditures other than those for social security, which are sacrosanct, and large reductions in defense expenditures will require fundamental and therefore unlikely changes in defense policy—changes which no president since World War II has been willing to make. Even if Congress were to eliminate public assistance, medicaid, employment, social services, and community programs, the budget would still show a big deficit. If President Bush is to reduce the deficit substantially, he will have to agree to higher taxes.

The two chief taxes by far are the personal income and the social insurance taxes. In 1987 they supplied as much as 81.3 percent of total revenues. Social insurance taxes include those for medicare as well as for old age, disability, and survivors' insurance (OASDI) (Table 8.2). Currently, employers are deducting 7.51 percent of wages to pay the social insurance taxes and contribute a matching amount.

Until 1988 the social insurance tax rate was 7.15 percent. Another increase would stir up much opposition among the young voters who must pay the tax, which represents a transfer of income from the young to the old. It will not be possible to maintain the fiction that the retired have purchased their benefits in a manner similar to that of purchasers of annuities. The beneficiaries are being paid out of current tax receipts. Moreover, their benefits far exceed what they would have received had their payments plus employers' contributions been invested. Indeed, the gain in their benefits resulting from the congressional decision early in the seventies to permit a cost-of-living allowance equal to the increase in the consumer price index has resulted in a faster rate of growth in the benefits than took place in workers' wages. The increase in the social security taxes in 1988 came about only because the funds for OASDI were nearly exhausted. To get even this increase, Reagan had to dodge the direct responsibility by appointing a special commission, which recommended raising the rate.

Not only would higher social security taxes arouse much opposition, but they would have bad effects. They would put unskilled workers out of their jobs, and many of them have been unemployed for months and years. Raising the cost of hiring them by raising social security taxes paid by employers will make matters worse. An employer can save labor costs by introducing automated equipment, which is more likely to displace unskilled than skilled labor.

Moreover, unless the law is changed, the use of social security tax revenues is restricted. Foreseeing what a tempting grab bag the huge accumulation of funds would be, President Roosevelt blocked the use of these for other purposes by requiring the revenues to be paid into trust funds.

Finally, as the population ages and medical advances continue to be made, the cost of medicare will grow. It would be overly optimistic to expect the current tax rate to continue to cover costs. Indeed, medicare funds already threaten to run out, and Congressman Claude Pepper and the American Association of Retired Persons (AARP) are demanding coverage for nursing home care. The charges at a low-cost nursing care facility easily exceed $20,000 per year. The average aged couple has to spend all their savings to qualify for medicaid. We can expect some broadening of the coverage provided by medicare to include at least part of the costs of nursing care. In short, an increase in the social insurance taxes will not take care of the deficit.

Raising the corporate income tax may provide a politically easy way out, since big corporations are a popular scapegoat. But we should not disregard the negative effects of high corporate income taxes. To avoid high taxes corporations will borrow: They will issue bonds, the interest on which is treated as a tax deductible expense. The alternative is to invest retained earnings or to issue stocks. The higher the corporate income tax rate is, the greater is the incentive for companies to finance their activities by piling up debts. As long as prosperity reigns, companies can gladly add to their borrowing. But when many companies are heavily in debt even a small recession may be dangerous. The firms that miss interest payments and go into bankruptcy will drag others after them. A small recession may get worse.

The individual income tax is an obvious possibility. A small rise in the rates, together with some reductions in expenditures and another small tax on consumption, would be enough to eliminate most of the deficit. Proposals are offered in Chapter 11. Under the new law we no longer have to fear that incentives of high-income taxpayers will be damaged. If they were still paying the top rate of 1980—70 percent—a rise might induce many investors not to incur risks that promise only small after-tax returns, highly paid executives would relax a bit, and they would spend more time huddled with accountants trying to avoid taxes. But the tax schedule now stops rising at much lower rates. Young lawyers will continue to work until midnight just as frequently when they have to pay out 35 percent of additional income as when the rate is 33 percent. Nor will a higher top rate in this range induce firms to sweeten executives' incomes by giving them a car plus unlimited entertainment allowances.

Thus a modest increase in the individual tax rates would contribute substantially to reducing the deficit without doing economic harm. Nevertheless, since the candidates for either party's presidential nomination, except for Governor Babbitt, did not dare to mention taxes, Congress may find even a small increase too hot to propose, to say nothing of enacting one, especially after the stock market crash and the fear of a recession.

What about excise taxes, which are included under "other"? These taxes, which punish the evils of smoking and drinking, produce a small fraction of the total revenue. Because the dissolute insist on their bad habits, these taxes already raise large revenues relative to the total sales of the products. Nevertheless, increases in these tax rates will do little to reduce the deficit.

Many newspaper editorials argue for an oil import tax, an apparently easy, painless remedy that would have the additional beneficial effects of destroying OPEC, encouraging oil conservation, and saving the domestic industry. But this is no free lunch. Taxing imports will raise the price of oil by the full amount of the tax. Suburban and rural drivers, who use many gallons of gasoline, will be very unhappy. Proponents conceal their real purpose, which is to protect domestic producers who will enjoy a great windfall. Taxing imports will have the negative effect of accelerating the exhaustion of domestic oil and increasing future dependency on foreign supplies. The alternative, which is to tax all gasoline, will hurt domestic as well as foreign producers. It will also raise car drivers' cost of living. However, a gasoline tax can produce large revenues. House Speaker Jim Wright may carry enough influence to block such a tax, and it is probably unrealistic to expect large enough revenues to take care of the deficit. However, a package of increased and new taxes that includes this one should not be ruled out.

General sales taxes appear to be strictly the turf of state and local governments. However, Washington tax circles frequently discuss a similar tax, the value-added tax (VAT), which is popular in Europe. The VAT is levied on the addition to value at each stage of production and distribution. The steel mill would pay to the IRS the VAT of, say, 3 percent on the difference between its receipts and its payments to other firms for materials, fuels, and electricity. This difference is the value added. Wages, salaries, interest on debt, and dividends would be included in the value added subject to the tax. The steel mill would include the VAT in its bills to customers. Each successive buyer who resold the steel after processing or distribution would do the same.

A VAT has not been enacted probably because it would hit the poor more than the rich, and a tax of 3 percent on all expenditures would be no small trifle for those at the economic bottom. The Democrats probably would refuse to sacrifice the traditional principle of progressive taxation. Some progressivity could be retained by exempting food and housing. Alternatively, payments could be made to the poor to reduce the burden—a negative income tax. But such efforts to limit the costs to the poor would have to be made up for by higher tax rates or by other taxes.

CONCLUSION

The impression of a great, difficult problem is false. We can afford easily to pay the higher taxes needed to eliminate the deficit. No harm would be done to the economy. A small rise in income tax rates would not affect incentives significantly. A small VAT and a small gasoline tax may have to be part of a politically acceptable package.

Reagan's ferocious opposition to tax increases prevented a solution of the deficit problem. When he entered office, the effect of a modest increase in personal income tax rates would have been larger than the same increase at present because the tax rates are lower, especially at the high end of the schedule.

To oppose tax increases Reagan relied also on the argument concerning government waste. David Stockman has reported numerous White House budgetary discussions dominated by slogans about bureaucratic waste,[4] and Reagan himself was not above making sarcastic remarks about welfare checks paying for liquor. The issue thus shifts to expenditures. Chapters 9 and 10 take up the issue of whether or not there is much room for trimming government expenditures without sacrificing useful projects or imposing hardships on the poor.

9

DEFENSE
EXPENDITURES

EXPENDITURES AND THE DEFICIT

Comparing the budgets of 1980 and 1987, we can see that most of
the increase in the deficit over this period was due to the rise in
expenditures. Although Reagan's deficit, which broke all records,
raised much more commotion, his predecessor's was already large.
In 1980 the deficit came to 2.2 percent of the GNP, compared to
3.4 percent in 1987; the difference was 1.2 percentage points. More
than half of this difference came from the growth of expenditures.
In 1987 expenditures came to 22.79 percent of the GNP, which was
0.70 percentage points greater than in 1980. This was the contribution of the growth of expenditures to the increase in the deficit.
The remainder was due to the reduction in tax rates.

The biggest increases in expenditures came in defense (Table 9.1).
The next largest increase was in interest payments—the inadvertent,
if inevitable, result of the increase in the public debt since 1980 and
also of the rise in the real interest rate. The growth in medicare
expenditures was due to the rising costs of medical services and the
growth in the number of elderly people, which also raised social
security expenditures. The rise in the cost-of-living allowance
(COLA) contributed to the increase in social security expenditures.
Efforts by the administration to keep the deficit down focused on
poverty assistance programs, including Aid to Families with Dependent Children (AFDC), community development, and public
housing, which resulted in the very large fall in "other" expendi-

Table 9.1
Federal Outlays as a Percentage of GNP,
1980 and 1987 Fiscal Years and the Change

	Percentage		Change (1987 minus 1980)
	1980	1987	
Total	22.1	22.8	0.7
National Defense	5.1	6.4	1.4
Social Security	4.4	4.7	0.3
Medicare	1.2	1.7	0.5
Interest	2.0	3.1	1.2
Other	9.5	6.8	-2.7

Source: Based on *Economic Report of the President 1988,* pp. 338–39.

tures as a percentage of GNP. Other expenditures in this category, which also fell sharply, included payments to state and local governments under "revenue sharing." The next chapter considers these nondefense expenditures in more detail.

The most obvious candidate for cuts in expenditures is defense. Past examinations of defense have revealed many wasteful expenditures, especially for weapons systems. Expenditures could be cut without abandoning strategic goals. But Congress will not approve a large reduction in expenditures without a change in policy. The elimination of waste alone would be insufficient.

Gorbachev's speech at the UN on December 7, 1988 will force the Bush administration to reevaluate the defense policy. The General Secretary committed the Soviets to a unilateral overall reduction in their conventional forces of 500,000, or 10 percent. The cuts promised in the forces in Eastern Europe and the western part of the Soviet Union were spelled out as follows: 50,000 troops, 10,000 tanks, 8,500 tanks, and 800 combat aircraft. In addition, Gorbachev promised to have the Warsaw Pact forces abandon their attack posture and adopt a defensive one.

Many Pentagon officials oppose making reciprocal cuts on the ground that the Soviets will continue to maintain superiority in Europe. They also say that Gorbachev will not last long. The Soviet bureaucrats, whose privileges are threatened by *perestroika*, will overthrow him. Gorbachev's successor will be less conciliatory to the West. The Pentagon, along with such past administration members as Kissinger and Brzezinski, insists that the current détente is a pause in the centuries-old Russian expansionism. Originating from the Muscovy region, the Russians conquered the huge empire that now is the Soviet Union plus Eastern Europe. Gorbachev's step back will be followed by two steps forward in the drive to conquer the entire Eurasian land mass. The Russians have great patience, and they will not give up their imperial ambitions. The West would be foolish to rest its hopes for peace on an apparent new Soviet *weltanschauung*. Moreover, Gorbachev is not the great new savior. The promise of arms cuts is the result of the poor performance of the Soviet economy and of the U.S. arms buildup. Gorbachev recognizes that the arms competition strains the Soviet economy. This is not the time to relent. This is the time to press the Soviets for more concessions. They should cut their forces further before NATO makes any reciprocal moves. The Warsaw Pact will still have superior forces in Europe unless they make further reductions. Moreover, the source of the East-West conflict is Soviet control over Eastern Europe. The United States should insist on a general Soviet withdrawal from the region before it agrees to reduce its own forces.

The comparative strength of NATO's and the Warsaw Pact's forces is an old issue. The Defense Department has argued for many years that the Warsaw Pact is much stronger, but many military experts disagree. NATO's function is to deter a Soviet attack. If the experts disagree on the relative strength of the two sides, then the Soviets cannot be certain of an easy victory. The prospect of a costly war is a sufficient deterrent. There need be no guarantee of a Soviet defeat to ensure peace.

True, Gorbachev may not remain in power, and his successor may be much less conciliatory. The superpowers then may resume their dangerous and costly arms race. One of the primary goals of the new administration should be to assist Gorbachev in retaining power. Not to respond to Gorbachev's overtures with reciprocal cuts in arms would give the signal to the Soviets that any efforts they might make to end the arms race are hopeless. The Soviets then will judge Gorbachev's peace effort a failure. The U.S. should reciprocate and help Gorbachev achieve success. Not to do so would undermine his position. Indeed, the hawks are malicious when they refuse to make concessions. They appear to want Gorbachev to fall and the Cold War to continue. Gorbachev has enemies whose good jobs are threatened by his economic reforms. So radical are his proposals that his own position may not be secure. He may fail and be overthrown if the West does not make a serious effort to assist him. The Bush administration should not miss this opportunity for an historic reduction in tensions and world danger. We should also recognize that Gorbachev has presented U.S. policymakers with an opportunity painlessly to reduce the federal deficit.

THE NUCLEAR DEFENSE POLICY

A decision to cut defense expenditures substantially would be a difficult one, for it would require revamping the policy pursued by all administrations since World War II. Reagan changed only the rhetoric, not the substance of policy, and while he raised expenditures, the increase was consistent with the decades-old policy. Reagan approved of the B–1 bomber and other expensive weapons programs, which Carter had rejected, but a large cut could come only with a dramatic reversal of policy. Moreover, if Carter had won a second term he might have raised defense expenditures as much as Reagan did. He agreed with Reagan on the MX, the Trident II, and the aircraft carrier programs. A large cut in defense expenditures could come only with a dramatic reversal of policy.

However, since the current defense posture is dangerous as well as expensive, a reversal is possible in the near future. A side-effect of the recent arms control agreement is less fear of an attack on Western Europe, and the Soviet leaders apparently are eager for a détente, if for no other reason than to reduce the cost of defense. The recent movements away from a centrally-directed economy toward a market economy suggest a concerted, radical effort to raise the Soviet standard of living. In addition, the Politburo may be permitting much more open discussion of social and economic issues. These changes should help to relieve East-West tensions.

The primary goal of our defense policy should be to reduce the risk of nuclear war. This goal is not as obvious as one might suppose. It conflicts with the goal of deterrence, which requires us to take some risk of a nuclear war breaking out. As the hawks see the problem, undue weight given to preventing a nuclear war would give the Soviets a blank check. To resist Soviet expansionism we must be prepared to stand firm in confrontations. The risk of nuclear war is the cost of preventing the Soviets from gaining imperial ends. This is the conflict of goals that divides hawks from doves. If we believe the hawks, the risk of deliberate Soviet aggression is high, and to deter an attack we must be prepared to take some risk of nuclear war. The doves, on the other hand, believe that the risk of war arising from the possession by both sides of weapons that can destroy the other side's land-based retaliatory capability is high—much higher than the risk of deliberate Soviet aggression. Deterrence does not rank high as a goal for the doves, since it entails superpower competition in the accumulation of first-strike weapons.

A defense policy that minimizes the risk of nuclear war may require larger expenditures than the alternative, which seeks deterrence. But we should not reject the primary goal for the sake of economy. Unfortunately, Truman chose the nuclear defense policy for economic reasons. Nuclear weapons were "cheaper" than adequate conventional forces. Eisenhower also preferred the less costly nuclear forces. But no economy is gained when the result is a higher risk of annihilation.

THE SOVIET THREAT

Why do we spend so much money on defense? First, the basic fear is that the Politburo seeks to control more territory, particularly Western Europe. We need a strong deterrent to prevent an invasion. Second, we fear that conventional and nuclear forces will fail to deter them if the Soviets can expect a victory in some sense or other. Policymakers foresee a sweep of Soviet conventional forces through Western Europe, or, alternatively, the destruction of land-based U.S. nuclear forces. Assured of one or the other kind of victory, a Soviet leader would proceed to invade Western Europe. Not all leaders are likely to be as friendly as Gorbachev is, and one may have greater imperialist dreams. Third, in a purely conventional war the Soviets will easily overrun Western Europe. Although the United States will reinforce its conventional forces in West Germany, NATO will resort to nuclear weapons early to prevent a Soviet conquest. These plans to use nuclear weapons follow from the fourth premise, which is that the prospect of a nuclear war is a better deterrent than of a conventional war, which the Soviets can win.

Not only do we need superior conventional land forces and nuclear forces to carry out this policy, but we also need a superior navy. In a war, the United States will have to ship additional forces, equipment, and supplies to NATO. The navy's principal task will be to protect the convoys against submarine attacks. The navy plans what is called the maritime strategy, which calls for attacking the submarines before they leave their base at Murmansk. A large aircraft carrier force will attack the base. The navy also anticipates ocean warfare independent of the land war in Europe. The United States will need aircraft carrier forces to maintain supremacy in all the oceans.

Reagan continued the 40-year-old defense policy. Truman helped organize NATO and committed the United States to defend Western Europe with nuclear and conventional forces. Under Eisenhower, the nuclear arsenal grew. Kennedy ordered the deployment of 1,000 Minuteman ICBMs. Under Johnson, Secretary McNamara directed the development of multiple independently-targeted re-entry vehicles (MIRVs) and the improvement of accuracy. Nixon ordered the deployment of the MIRVed Minuteman IIIs. Carter proposed the deployment of 200 10-warhead, highly accurate MX missiles. Congress did not agree. Reagan was able to get Congress to agree to the deployment of 50 MX missiles. Over the whole postwar period the alleged superiority of Soviet conventional forces supported the United States nuclear buildup. The "missile gap" was Kennedy's vehicle to the presidency and justified his Minuteman program. The development and deployment of MIRVed ICBMs came while the Soviets were rapidly building their ICBM arsenal. Carter built his case for the MX on the Soviet capability of destroying the U.S. land-based capability. The same argument justified Reagan's insistence on the MX, the Trident II, and the Strategic Defense Initiative (SDI) programs.

We would not give a hoot for superiority unless we feared the Soviet bogey.[1] The prospect of a *deliberate* Soviet attack is the ultimate justification of the continued defense buildup. I emphasize the word "deliberate" because deterrence is effective only against such an attack. American policy has sought to minimize the Aggression Risk (AR), or the probability of deliberate Soviet aggression. The buildup of nuclear forces along with conventional forces achieves this purpose.

The defense policy increases the other, greater risk—the Preemption Risk (PR)—by enhancing the counterforce capability and provoking matching Soviet efforts. Each side seeks the capability of destroying the other's nuclear forces quickly enough to preempt an attack. With MIRVing and greater accuracy, both sides' counterforce capabilities have increased. The growth has raised the danger of a preemptive attack in a crisis when the leaders of both sides fear destruction by the other. Crises will recur from time to time. For example, in a revolution Iranian communists may gain control of a region and invite Soviet assistance. West Germany may set off a general war by intervening in a revolt in East Germany. Even crises over minor issues are dangerous because, expecting future conflicts, each superpower seeks to impress the other with its resolve to resort to nuclear weapons. The very destructiveness of the nuclear weapons reduces their credibility and their power as a deterrent. Since each superpower fears that the other will doubt its resolve, they may take greater risks than in a similar conflict in the prenuclear era. Thus, a nuclear war may break out without deliberate Soviet aggression. Moreover., in a crisis false signals of a nuclear launch may frighten one side to launch an actual attack. The deterrent does not reduce the risk of nuclear war arising from a game of chicken over a minor conflict or from false signals. This is the Preemption Risk of a nuclear war. The PR increases with the counterforce capability. The MX will reduce the AR but it will increase the PR. Since it is the latter risk that is greater, the defense policy increases the danger of war.

A popular argument for the current policy is that no president since Truman has deviated from it. If the premises were false, presumably, administrations would not have been so consistent. But age and consistency does not prove validity. The Soviet bogey was Truman's and Acheson's deliberate fabrication aimed at gaining congressional support for aid to the Greek government against a communist-led revolt in 1947. Truman and Acheson cooked up the specter of a huge Red Army poised for attack on the West despite intelligence reports that the Soviets were too exhausted to conduct a major war and would be for a long time. The problem was that the Congress, dominated by penny-pinchers, would not vote the necessary appropriations to stop the Soviets from taking over Greece without a big scare. So Truman and Acheson invented the bogey, which survives to this day.

Dulles built up the bogey with his attacks on the godless totalitarians. But the godless and totalitarian Soviet leaders were not ready for a major war. The Berlin Crisis of 1949 did not portend an attack on the West; Stalin's intention was to stop the buildup of another great German military power that would join an anti-Soviet alliance. Nor did Khrushchev set off the Berlin crises of 1958 and 1961 to test the West's will preparatory to an invasion. It was no secret even at the time that he wanted to preserve an economically viable East Germany. Soviet control of West Berlin would close off the escape hatch through which thousands of East Germans were escaping to the West.

Kennedy rode to victory in the 1960 election on the Soviet bogey. According to Kennedy, the Soviets instigated the Third World civil wars in their pursuit of world power. He attacked the Eisenhower administration for allowing the "missile gap," which turned out to be fictitious. Kennedy exploited the communist menace to win votes more than any other presidential candidate before or since. He represented the Eisenhower administration as lethargic in the face of the threat. Although he had learned that there was no missile gap, immediately on entering office he ordered the deployment of 1,000 Minuteman ICBMs. At the time the Soviets had only four.[2]

For Kennedy, each crisis was a test of his will to use the nuclear weapons. Of all the nuclear-era presidents, he was the most dangerous. He risked war over Berlin and over the deployment of missiles in Cuba to demonstrate his resolve. He believed that if the Soviets suspected that he lacked resolve they would march on Western Europe. But neither the Berlin nor the Cuban Crises came about because the Soviets were planning an invasion. We have mentioned the origin of the Berlin Crisis of 1961. In Cuba the Soviets were attempting to gain a retaliatory nuclear capability. American aircraft at West European bases could attack the Soviet Union, which lacked a defense.

The Kennedy buildup provoked a nuclear arms race. The Soviets sought to catch up; the United States developed and deployed

MIRVed Minuteman IIIs. The Soviets followed suit with SS–18s and SS–9s. Succeeding administrations interpreted the buildup as a further effort by the Soviets to gain world dominance, not as part of a race initiated by the United States.

Kennedy, Dulles, and Nitze (in his early years) advanced the theory that the oppressive dictatorship sought to relieve the strains with provocative actions that risked war. External threats, which the leaders themselves provoked, justified the oppressive rule. What was more, the communists admitted to the goal of wiping out capitalism.

In recent years, Henry Kissinger, Zbigniew Brzezinski, Harold Brown, and Paul Nitze justified the defense policy by ascribing expansionist ambitions to the Politburo. They rehashed old historical arguments. Heirs of the tsars, the Politburo acquired the ambition of conquering the entire Eurasian land mass. According to Brzezinski, the Russians proper, who are the descendants of early inhabitants of Muscovy, took control of the vast expanse of what was to become the Soviet Union over a period beginning in the seventeenth century. The Afghanistan War is the most recent expression of this expansionist drive. Other expressions since World War II include the occupation of Eastern Europe, the threat against West Berlin, the Greek Civil War, and demands by Stalin for a share of the control of the Dardanelles. The hawks use routine, boilerplate arguments in defense of the MX program; the Scowcroft Commission, appointed by Reagan, argued that the autocratic Soviet rulers required a military threat to preserve their control. This was the rationale for the MX. We needed the weapon to deter aggressive acts intended to divert the attention of the Soviet people from their condition.

The references to the original Russians and the tsars are not persuasive. Moreover, being communist does not make the Soviet rulers eager to undertake the huge costs of a major, conventional war, whether or not they expect an ultimate victory, to say nothing of risking nuclear annihilation. Communist propaganda against capitalism does not signify serious aggressive intentions any more than Reagan's condemnation of communism does. Soviet expansionist ambitions provide a less plausible explanation of the post-World War II crises than do the alternative ones suggested above. The fear of another invasion by a revived Germany at some later date probably motivated Stalin's insistence on maintaining control over Eastern Europe. Roosevelt and Churchill initially planned to raze the enemy's industry after the war to put an end to the recurrent German threat. The impossibility of an agricultural Germany sustaining itself led them to cancel the plan. Nor does the continued occupation of Eastern Europe signify a Soviet threat, for free governments there may join NATO in an anti-Soviet military alliance. The continued occupation is a defensive measure.

It is doubtful that Soviet leaders would undertake the high costs or take huge risks to fulfill hegemonic ambitions. They may support leftist Third World revolutions and assist communist governments out of imperialist as well as ideological motives. Moreover, the Soviets gain military advantages from communist successes. They have established naval bases in Vietnam and Somália that may supply submarines in time of war. But such assistance, which is relatively cheap, does not herald an attack on the well-armed West. The Soviets will compete with the United States for Third World support, but this rivalry should be distinguished from a threat to the West. Kissinger and Brzezinski have advocated a powerful nuclear arsenal on the dubious grounds that the side perceived as the most powerful will win world leadership. Other ways of gaining influence are less costly and dangerous.

Policy is so much in thrall to the fear of a Soviet attack that one would think that most Sovietologists had raised the alarm. Yet such prominent experts as Adam B. Ulam, Thomas W. Wolfe, Joseph L. Nogee, Robert H. Donaldson, David Holloway, Robin Edmonds, and Marshall D. Shulman, who have studied the Soviet government for years, have avoided making dire predictions.[3] They do say that the Red Army will not leave an occupied region and that the Soviets will support Third World revolutions. However, they do not suggest that the West is in danger.

Before undertaking a major conventional war, the Kremlin would have to prepare its public and thus show its hand. It could not secretly prepare the large forces required for an attack and suddenly launch one. A secretly-prepared and sudden nuclear attack is possible, but our nuclear forces are an adequate deterrent. The issue thus concerns the likelihood of a Soviet conventional attack. Unlike Hitler in the thirties, the Soviet leaders have not stirred up the masses. On the contrary, under Brezhnev the Kremlin welcomed détente, and currently Gorbachev pursues a new rapprochement. The routine, hackneyed diatribes against capitalism seek only to legitimize the Kremlin's bureaucratic, oppressive rule. The prosperous, well-paid bureaucrats, who have easy access to Western goods, need an excuse for exploiting the public. The Soviet people learn in one way or another that West Europeans do not wait in line for hours for supplies of fruit and vegetables and that many can afford to buy cars, television sets, and so on. To show the Soviets how much better off they are than the people of the West, the press describes the poverty of the South Bronx, blaming the greed of the capitalists. We need not fear aggressive intentions.

For the danger of an invasion of Western Europe to justify the high Preemption Risk entailed by the nuclear buildup, the Soviets must be greedy enough for extending their domain to risk their own destruction. No U.S. administration has addressed this issue directly. Weinberger did not say that the Soviets will attack Western Europe within the next 10 years unless we acquired the MX, another aircraft carrier, the B-1B bomber, and more attack submarines. The justification has depended heavily on comparisons between Soviet and U.S. defense expenditures and on old history. These arguments do not address the crucial question: What is the probability of a deliberate Soviet attack on Western Europe within 10 years? Ten years is arbitrary, but any period selected should be short enough for the answer to matter and for a reasonable estimate to be possible. In any case, a difference of a few years should not affect the conclusion. If the probability is high, then the next question is: What is the most effective way of reducing this risk? Despite the vast sums spent on preparing for such an attack, no policymaker has declared that the probability is high. And this is not surprising, with the evidence as dubious as it is.

Proponents of the MX, the Pershing IIs, and so on assume that the probability of a Soviet attack is high if the Politburo can expect a victory of some kind. Former NATO Commander General Bernard Rogers opposed the withdrawal of the Pershing IIs from West Germany because NATO could not repel a Soviet conventional invasion without resorting to nuclear weapons. He simply assumed that they would attack at some time soon. Discussing a vague, indefinite future is of little value. Many things will change. Eastern Europe may achieve greater independence. China is emerging as a great power. Western Europe may choose to rely on its own defense and less on U.S. forces. Technological changes in defense may tilt the balance of strength. Rogers' pessimism about the prospects of war in the near future is not shared by all defense experts; some have argued that the Soviets cannot expect an easy victory.[4] The costs will be enormous, and a conventional war may blow up into a nuclear war. Such uncertainty is enough to deter an invasion. No persuasive evidence has shown sufficiently intense Soviet imperialist ambitions for the Politburo to undertake the costs and risks of a major war.

The next major issue is that of superiority. For the moment, we will accept the assumption that the Soviets are greedy for more empire. Relying heavily on comparisons between the levels of Soviet and U.S. defense expenditures and more particularly on the trends, the Defense Department has concluded that the Soviet forces are overwhelmingly stronger. However, concerning expenditure levels, the appropriate comparison is between the NATO countries as a group and the Warsaw Pact countries. All comparisons between these two totals favor the NATO group.

The Defense Department has claimed that the Soviets were racing ahead—that their defense expenditures were growing much more rapidly than our own. Recent estimates by the CIA for the Soviet Union, which show much smaller increases than earlier ones, fail to support the claim. In 1983 the CIA reduced its estimate for the period 1976 to 1981 of growth rates of 3 to 5 percent to 2 percent or less. The greatest alarm had been over the growth of the stock of weapons, which the CIA also had estimated to be from 3 to 5 percent. In 1983 this estimate came down to 0 to 1 percent.[5] The Defense Department refused to acknowledge the new estimates before 1985, and even then it warned against the earlier large accumulations and the continuing rapid growth of Soviet military research and development.[6]

The Defense Department was still busily trying to hold together the Soviet bogey, without which the policy of accumulating a large counterforce arsenal could not be sustained.

I may be wrong about the Soviet threat. My reading of the history of the postwar period may have led me to underestimate the threat. Reagan may have been right, and the Soviets may not have pressed harder to realize their imperialist dreams only because we have had strong defenses. It is difficult to interpret the intentions of the other side in a two-sided hostile relationship. Nevertheless, we can judge only from the historical record, and the evidence suggests that our policy has been based on an exaggerated threat. To minimize even an uncertain threat we might still have wanted to build a powerful counterforce arsenal, were it not for the tradeoff between minimizing the Aggression and Preemption Risks. Constructing a powerful arsenal capable of destroying the Soviet retaliatory arsenal minimized the Aggression Risk at the cost of increasing the Preemption Risk. Judging the available evidence, the latter risk is far the greater one. Unfortunately, policymakers must make decisions under uncertainty; they cannot wait for final, certain answers. Therefore, the primary goal of policy should be to minimize the Preemption Risk.

DEFENSE EXPENDITURES

It will not be possible for the Bush administration to reduce the deficit substantially by cutting only defense expenditures without withdrawing a large portion of the U.S. forces now in Europe. If we had withdrawn completely before 1986, total conventional defense expenditures that year would have been cut by $124 billion—about 52 percent. Assuming that expenditures for nuclear defense were maintained, this would have resulted in a reduction of 42 percent in total military expenditures.[7] This reduction would have gone a long way toward eliminating the deficit.

The participation by the United States in the defense of Western Europe has spoiled its governments. They can bear the cost of an adequate conventional defense without U.S. assistance. The argument that they cannot do so stems from the false premise that a defense is adequate only if it is certain of repelling an invasion. Certainty is unnecessary for deterrence. The costs of a major war, whatever outcome the Soviets forecast, will deter them from initiating one.

Other withdrawals also are prudent. The South Koreans can defend themselves against the North Koreans without U.S. troops on the scene. Eliminating the expense of the defense of South Korea would reduce the defense budget by 7 percent.

Thus, expenditures can be cut without threatening national security even if we assume that the Soviets pose a threat. The rejection of the bogey does not imply that there will be no confrontations. Nor does it imply that defense expenditures can be cut to zero. What it means is that policymakers have exaggerated the threat. Crises will recur, and the United States will need some defense to protect its interests.

The available big economies are in expenditures for personnel and for weapons for conventional defense. Nuclear defense expenditures are too small to promise big savings. In 1987, 11 percent of the budget provided funds for the nuclear forces.[8] The allocation was this large because additions were being made. A much smaller percentage of the defense expenditures were for the operation and maintenance of the existing system.

Thus, if we do reduce the size of the nuclear forces it will be because they are dangerous, not because they are costly. The battle against the MX is motivated by the fear that a large number will raise the Preemption Risk, not by the expense. Cutting expenditures on nuclear weapons will not do much for the deficit.

Cost should not be an element in the choice between a nuclear and a conventional defense system. If policy continues to assume that the danger of a Soviet attack is high, then provision should be made for an adequate conventional defense even if this should require larger expenditures. Asserting that the danger is high unless the United States is prepared to rely on nuclear weapons is equivalent to saying that, given the present deployment of conventional forces on both sides, the Soviets will attack within some short period. In that case, the West should proceed to build conventional forces that are certain to repel a Soviet conventional attack.

The United States should be prepared to rely on conventional forces plus a retaliatory nuclear capability. It should not add a strong counterforce capability, and it should fulfill the INF agreement and remove its Pershing IIs from West Germany. These dangerous weapons, which can strike Soviet missile silos and command posts within six to 10 minutes of launching, add to the Preemption Risk. The SLBMs, which do not threaten the Soviet arsenal, do not; they can be maintained as a retaliatory force to deter a Soviet nuclear strike. The MX and Trident II programs, which will threaten a first strike, should be abandoned.

In addition, the Strategic Defense Initiative (SDI) should also be

Table 9.2
Percentage Distribution of Administration's
Defense Budget Outlays for 1989
by Major Accounts

Military Personnel	27.4
Operation and Maintenance	29.1
Procurement	28.2
Research, development, test, and evaluation	12.4
Other	3.0
Total	100.0

Source: Based on Congressional Budget Office, *An Analysis of the President's Budgetary Proposals for Fiscal Year 1989,* March 1988, p. 34.

abandoned. It is widely agreed that no defense of cities will be possible in the foreseeable future. The program may be able to achieve a defense of missile bases. But such a defense is equivalent to adding to the nuclear forces; it adds to the threat to the Soviet retaliatory forces and thus to the Preemption Risk.

Some defense policymakers have proposed the withdrawal of U.S. troops from Western Europe without abandoning the Soviet bogey. Former West German Chancellor Helmut Schmidt, Henry Kissinger, and Zbigniew Brzezinski recently have made statements favoring the return of NATO's U.S. forces. Schmidt believes that the withdrawal would force Western Europeans to take on the responsibility for their own defense. Kissinger and Brzezinski, who no longer fear a threat to Western Europe, now assign a higher priority to deterring a Soviet invasion of Iran or other places in the Middle East. In a crisis troops would be more easily available for deployment outside Europe were they not already stationed there. The administration needs greater flexibility than it now has. Kissinger and Brzezinski also agree with Schmidt that NATO now can supply an adequate defense even without U.S. troops.

Table 9.2 presents the defense budget for 1988 broken down by major components. The three largest categories are military personnel, operation and maintenance (O & M), and procurement. Reagan won support for larger defense expenditures because of the fear that NATO's conventional forces lacked the strength and readiness to withstand a Soviet invasion. However, the services did not spend the additional billions for these purposes, which would be reflected by increases under the first two headings in Table 8.1. Instead, the money went to procurement. In fiscal year 1980, Carter spent $50.1 billion (1988 dollars) on procurement for the services. Under Reagan, budget authorizations went up every year reaching a peak of $100.6 billion in 1985. Authorizations have dropped off since, but not greatly. In fiscal 1988 the amount authorized was $80.9 billion. The services exploited the bonanza to acquire new weapons, knowing that in periods of stringency Congress would refuse to authorize the expenditures. Some of the new weapons were of dubious military value but were acquired simply because the services had vast sums suddenly made available. The additional funds allowed the services to go far down the list of items that they wanted to those that added little or nothing to the defensive capability of the forces. The services expect that when emergencies arise the money will be found for repairs, ammunition, and training. As a result, readiness tends to deteriorate.

The second reason is that preparation of the budget is guided by an arbitrary overall limit set in terms of aggregate percentage increases. It is not based on a detailed description by the services of their needs, which can be evaluated by the Office of Management and the Budget (OMB) and by congressional committees. Instead, as David Stockman has described, the then new Reagan administration decided before any detailed discussions with the Joint Chiefs of Staff (JCS) that defense expenditures would be raised 7 percent per year after allowing for price increases. Again, this number did not reflect an assessment of unmet needs. Stockman reports that it was set only to show that the Republicans were more concerned with defense than the Democrats. The outgoing Carter administration had planned an annual rate of increase of 5 percent—this too was a political number—and the Republicans had to do better.[9] The Pentagon then was asked to supply a list of needs that would fall within the allowed budget for each of the next five years.

As Stockman complains, the Pentagon came up with ridiculous demands. The acquisition of "administrative vehicles" was to rise from 2,000 to 18,000 per year. The army got the Bradley Fighting Vehicles at $1.7 million each, and the budget called for 7,000 of them. According to Stockman, the vehicle was a combination battlefield personnel carrier and tank, carrying a 25-mm. gun and missiles. Not only was it expensive, but it was vulnerable. The budget also called for 1,000 F–18 fighters, at a cost of $30 billion. The aircraft was originally planned to displace the navy's F–14 and the marines' AV–8B. The additional funds being available, the navy acquired the F–18 without giving up the F–14.[10]

Moreover, the procurement account reflects important and questionable policy decisions, even if we accept their basic premises. The 1989 budget plans large procurement outlays for the navy to implement what has become known as the maritime strategy. The navy is to spend $9.4 billion on aircraft, $4.6 billion on weapons, $10.3 billion on new ships and the conversion of older ships, and $6.8 billion for other items—a total of $31.1 billion.[11] This expenditure comes after the navy had spent $186 billion for procurement between 1982 and 1988.[12]

The maritime strategy, which calls for 15 aircraft carrier groups and a 600-ship navy, can be evaluated from the standpoint of the commitment to defend Western Europe. For NATO to conduct a conventional defense for more than a few months, the navy would have to protect Atlantic convoys against submarine attacks. The Reagan administration has supported the navy's offensive strategy of destroying Soviet submarines at their base at Murmansk. In his review of the 1987 defense budget for the Brookings Institution, Joshua Epstein concluded that a 15-carrier fleet would fail to accomplish this mission. At the minimum, 20 carriers and their associated forces would be needed. Epstein estimated the cost of a carrier battle group to be $18 billion; the five additional groups would entail a cost of $90 billion.[13]

The alternative defensive strategy would be far less expensive and more likely to succeed. The navy would concentrate its forces near the gaps between Greenland, Iceland, and the United Kingdom. Soviet submarines would have to survive this gauntlet before attacking heavily guarded convoys.

Not only was the Reagan administration's strategy expensive and unlikely to succeed, it was also dangerous. Offensive operations intended to destroy Soviet ballistic missile submarines (SSBNs) risk triggering a nuclear war. The plan is to minimize the risk of nuclear retaliation by relying only on conventional weapons. Nevertheless, with their retaliatory capability threatened, the Soviets may disregard such restraint. Not only will they fear the destruction of this capability, but they may expect a first strike. The offensive strategy also invites a nuclear war by deploying such large, lucrative targets as aircraft carriers.

The expensive maritime strategy has diverted billions from better strategies. If the Soviets do attack, they will attempt to overwhelm NATO's ground forces quickly with their masses of tanks. NATO's defenses against such an attack may require more manpower, tanks, antitank guided missiles, fortifications, and close support aircraft.

The navy continues to acquire Trident submarines and missiles. The total cost of the Trident II missiles is estimated at $38 billion. The Trident II SLBMs, which will have a high accuracy, are particularly dangerous. Together with the MX missiles, these weapons will render much of the Soviet land-based retaliatory force vulnerable. We will return to this subject later.

In fiscal year 1989 the air force plans to spend $33.2 billion for the procurement of aircraft, missiles, and other items. The expenditures will include those for the B–1 bomber, the Stealth bomber, and the MX.[14] It is estimated that the cost of the planned force of 50 MXs will be $30 billion. The theory is that these additions will deter a Soviet strategic attack. Without the enlarged arsenal, the Soviets may be able to wipe out the U.S. land-based arsenal. The SLBMs will be an ineffective deterrent, since they can destroy only cities. A president may refuse to order retaliation by SLBMs out of fear of inviting the destruction of our own cities. This is also why we are replacing the Poseidons with the much more accurate Trident IIs. The Defense Department urges the deployment of the MX and the Trident II to provide a time-urgent counterforce capability. These accurate weapons will have the capability of striking Soviet land-based missiles within 30 minutes of launching. These weapons are essential for deterrence, according to the Defense Department, because they will enable the president to respond to an attack in a limited, selective manner. The threat of destruction of cities is not credible and thus is ineffective.

However, the MXs will not add much to the deterrent. In 1983 the Congressional Budget Office (CBO) estimated how many of the 100 MXs that the administration then requested would survive a Soviet attack. It assumed an attack after warning, and, following U.S. policy, that the missiles would not be launched prior to a strike or during an attack.[15] The estimates were for 1990, when the administration planned to have deployed 100 MX missiles, replacing the same number of Minuteman IIIs, eight Trident Is, and four Trident IIs. The bomber force was to have acquired 100 B-lBs. The pre-attack inventory was expected to include 450 Minuteman IIs, 450 Minuteman IIIs, 100 MXs, 31 Poseidons, 8 Trident Is, 4 Trident IIs, and 357 bombers.[16] The administration's program would increase the total number of surviving warheads by 65 percent from a 1983 level of 6,000 to 9,900. The number of surviving hard-target warheads would increase from 1,400 to 3,900, and prompt hard-target warheads from 150 to 180, not including the Trident II warheads, and to 890 including these warheads. The vulnerable MX missiles would add little to the surviving capability. Since a major strike would destroy all but 10 percent of the MX missiles, they would contribute only 1 percent of the surviving warheads and 3 percent of the hard-target warheads, including those on Trident IIs.[17] Since the plans now call for 50 MXs instead of the 100 that the CBO anticipated, these last two numbers should be divided by two.

The acquisition of the 50 MXs and the Trident IIs will add to the Preemption Risk, since they increase considerably the United States' first-strike capability. The CBO estimates that by the year 2000, when 20 Trident submarines will be deployed, the number of hard-target warheads will be 6,800, including 4,800 on Trident IIs and 500 on MXs. This increase represents a quadrupling of the current inventory of hard-target warheads, and the Trident II and MX warheads will be much more accurate than those on hand. All the current Soviet ICBMs will be vulnerable.[18]

If few MXs can survive a Soviet attack, then it appears that their real but unacknowledged purpose is to threaten a launch on warning or even during a crisis before a warning. But such a threat will greatly increase the Preemption Risk. In any crisis, a false signal of an attack or the misinterpretation of communications among Soviet command stations, which are detected by the United States, may cause a launch. The MXs also will raise the risk in a crisis of a Soviet attack prompted by false signals of an attack and the misinterpretation of communications among American posts.

The air force's procurement budget includes expenditures for the construction of B-1B bombers to replace the present B-52s. Manned bombers have advantages over missiles; they can be recalled, and they can take off on warning of a Soviet attack. However, in a war their main task will be to carry air-launched cruise missiles (ALCMs), which they will launch several hundred miles from their targets. The B-1B advantage over the B-52 in being able to penetrate Soviet defenses will not be needed. The great expense of deploying a new manned bomber to carry ALCMs when the present bombers can perform just as well is unnecessary.

The procurement account is the best place to look for large economies. Decisions on procurement have been largely left to the services themselves, and their choices are not necessarily the best ones from the standpoint of overall strategy. These decisions are not always carefully reviewed by knowledgeable and disinterested civilians.

The research, development, test, and evaluation (RDT & E) account provides opportunities for savings. This account pays for the Strategic Defense Initiative (SDI), which is seeking to develop defenses against strategic attacks. The attempt to develop a defense of cities is hopeless, according to most independent scientists who have evaluated the program. Any such defense would have to be nearly perfect to be effective, and there are numerous ways in which the Soviets could retaliate to preserve their retaliatory capability— which they would have to do to protect themselves against a first strike or the threat of one. They could destroy space-based systems that would be part of a defense. Their missiles could be redesigned to make them less vulnerable. Once the missiles are in space and on the way to their targets, they are less likely to be struck by defending missiles, particularly when they are accompanied by numerous decoys.

But a terminal earth-based defense of missile bases is technologically possible. It need not be perfect to be effective, since even a partial defense will raise the cost of an attack. Judging the effectiveness of the technology becomes a matter of evaluating the relative costs of offense and defense. However, even assuming that a defensive system is expected to be successful in that sense, it is not clear that one should be deployed. It may increase the Preemption Risk in a crisis, not reduce it. The Soviets may fear that the United

States will launch an attack, expecting minimal damage from the retaliatory attack against its defended missile bases. This expectation may give them an incentive to launch their own first strike. An attack by a complete arsenal against defended bases is likely to inflict more damage than a second strike by surviving missiles. Soviet fears will be even greater if the defense system is coupled with the planned MX and Trident II forces.

If both sides proceed to deploy defensive systems, it will merely mean an accelerated arms race. Strategically, neither side will gain an advantage. Costs will rise to a new height, and the richer United States will suffer less. Supporters of the SDI hope that the United States will gain a lead in the race. Such hopes have led us down dangerous paths in the past, and there is no reason to expect the Soviets to lag for very long. Such hopes motivated the development of the atom bomb, the hydrogen bomb, MIRVs, and greater accuracy, but these hopes were disappointed.

Research funds are also devoted to the development of the Midgetman, a new land-based, single-warhead, mobile missile. This missile is expected to be less vulnerable than the stationary ICBMs because it will be mobile, and the incentive to use it in a first strike will be smaller than with MIRVed missiles. A single Midgetman will be able to destroy only a single Soviet ICBM, unlike the MX, which will destroy several. However, it will be expensive. For many of them to be moving about, a large empty region will be needed, and a large number of crews must be available to keep them moving. In addition, it is not clear that the gain in invulnerability will be significant. They cannot be placed in underground, hardened shelters, and their armor will provide little protection against a high-altitude nuclear explosion that will destroy objects over a large area. Moreover, if they are vulnerable, then there will be an incentive to fire them before they are destroyed. The Preemption Risk may remain the same, particularly if they carry as many warheads as the missiles they displace.

Another expensive project is developing the Stealth bomber, which will have a greater penetration capability than the B–1B. The bomber will be able to evade detection by Soviet defenses. However, there is little need for a manned bomber to penetrate Soviet defenses when ALCMs can be launched from points out of the reach of those defenses. Moreover, the ALCMs are relatively cheap and can strike within a smaller radius of their targets than manned bombers can.

We turn to the military personnel and the operation and maintenance (O&M) accounts, where there is little room for economies. If the pay scales are cut, the services will not attract men and women with enough education to handle the complex weapons and other equipment now being used. If we try to reduce the number of personnel, we will raise the risk of nuclear war by increasing our dependence on nuclear weapons. Moreover, we have increased our commitments without any increase in strength. The number of persons on active duty has remained at 2.1 million since the Vietnam War. In the same period, we have become more deeply involved in the troubles in the Middle East. The Reagan administration intervened in the Iran-Iraq War that ended in 1988 to protect oil tankers in the Persian Gulf. Should the Soviets intervene in a possible future Iranian civil war, the United States may want to land troops to prevent them from gaining control over the oil sources in the Middle East. In addition, to cut the number of personnel significantly, the Defense Department would have to put ships, aircraft, missiles, and so on, that Congress decided to acquire in past years into dead storage.

For similar reasons we cannot expect to reduce the expenditures for O&M. To its credit, the Reagan administration has not neglected readiness. If our main concern is to reduce the risk of being forced to resort to nuclear weapons in a war, then we should maintain large supplies of ammunition to prevent such a desperate measure.

Nor does the "other" category provide much opportunity for savings. Much of the funds are spent on military construction and for housing personnel, both in the United States and abroad. Expenditures for storing nuclear waste from naval vessels also come out of these funds. This account also pays for research and production programs by the Department of Energy for nuclear weapons and materials.

The proposed large changes in defense expenditures require a major change in policy, for which neither party is ready. However, a large number of small changes may be made. The Defense Department has been profligate in its recent period of expansiveness. Opportunities for canceling or slowing down procurement and other programs have been suggested by the CBO. The agency has suggested the cancellation of the F–15 fighter, the army helicopter improvement, the Aquila remotely piloted vehicle, the V–22 aircraft, the E–6 aircraft, the advanced medium-range air-to-air missile, and the Bradley fighting vehicle programs. The CBO has proposed slowing down the development of an advanced tactical fighter and reducing the funding for supporting equipment, which include cars, trucks, office equipment, for carrier battle groups, for the improvement of B–52s, for the tactical air force, and for military construction. The CBO also proposes reduction in expenditures for the MX, Trident II, and for RDT&E programs, including the SDI. The adoption of these proposals would have resulted in a reduction in the total budget of less than $14 billion in fiscal 1988,[19] or only 4.8 percent of total defense expenditures. The proposed changes will reduce the deficit at its current level by only 9 percent, or $150 billion.

Nor do the reductions in defense expenditures proposed by Epstein for the Brookings Institution add up to a significant cut. Epstein proposes the cancellation of the Midgetman and the Antisatellite programs, capping the MX program at 50 missiles and reducing its testing program, freezing SDI expenditures at the 1986 level, and not continuing the development of the Stealth bomber. The adoption of these proposals for fiscal 1988 would have reduced the budget authority for that year by $8.3 billion and outlays by only $2.2 billion.[20]

Nor is the sum of the savings in conventional programs that Epstein suggests much larger. The list of proposals is as follows: cancellation of the carrier service life extension program, of the procurement funds for the SSN–21 attack submarine, of the V–22 aircraft program, of the LHX helicopter program, of the Bradley fighting vehicle program, of the F–19 aircraft program, and of the C–17 aircraft program; denying funding for two nuclear aircraft carriers; reducing the funds for the navy's F–14 and A–6 aircraft for the existing aircraft carrier groups, for the DDG–51 destroyer, the CG–47 cruiser, the SSN–688 nuclear attack submarine, the TAO fleet oiler programs; reducing the funding for the Patriot air defense missile, for the F–15 aircraft, for follow-on forces attack/ deep attack programs; freezing the funding at the 1987 level of the advanced tactical fighter and the advanced medium-range air-to-air missile programs. Epstein also believes that the funding of O&M could be altered to yield savings. On the other hand, Epstein proposes to increase the rate of spending on certain other conventional programs. Together, these proposals would add up to a reduction in the budget authority for 1988 of $13.9 billion. In outlays, the saving would be a mere $4.8 billion.[21]

Despite all the talk about waste in defense spending, even what some would consider drastic pruning does not yield a large saving. The defense budget reflects the policy, and unless the policy is changed, we are not going to see a large cut. The deficit cannot be blamed on waste and inefficiency in the Defense Department.

10
OTHER FEDERAL EXPENDITURES

REAGAN'S EXPENDITURE CUTS

To evaluate the possibilities for cuts in nondefense federal expenditures, we shall review those made by the Reagan administration.

Following two decades of rapid economic growth and looking forward to the close of the Vietnam War, in the early seventies Congress was positively buoyant. While over the entire decade real GNP grew by 32 percent, real nondefense expenditures went up by 91 percent. The money did not come from higher tax rates. It came from lower defense expenditures, which fell from a peak of 8 percent of GNP to 4.9 percent; the growth in the GNP; and from inflation. Inflation imposed a nondeliberate tax. As individuals' nominal incomes rose with inflation, they entered higher tax brackets requiring them to pay a higher proportion of their income even though their real incomes were no higher. They were no better off, but the tax schedule did not discriminate between real and nominal increases in income. Indeed, in real terms workers' pretax earnings were no higher at the end of the decade than at the beginning.

Reagan had to seek economies to fulfill his campaign promises of lower taxes and a balanced budget. Certain groups of expenditure were protected. These included defense, interest payments, social security benefits, veterans' benefits, civil service pensions, and farmers' subsidies. Reagan had promised to raise defense expenditures, interest payments had to go on, and the elderly and the other groups of beneficiaries of congressional largesse were strong politically. He was forced to cut unprotected expenditures deeply. In the end, it was the poor, who lacked political power, who were the ones that suffered most.

According to Reagan, the monster eating up government revenues was waste and inefficiency. But outside defense, where the monster was untouchable, the potential savings were small because most of the nondefense budget went out in checks to the elderly, the poor, veterans, farmers, bondholders, and to former federal employees as pensions and disability benefits.

Adding it all up, Reagan did not cut total nondefense expenditures enough to prevent them from growing by 17 percent between 1980 and 1987. They went up at nearly the same rate as the real GNP, which grew by 20 percent.

SOCIAL SECURITY AND MEDICARE

The biggest nondefense expenditures are for social insurance, which includes old age pensions, medicare, and unemployment insurance (Table 10.1).

In the early seventies Congress had been generous to the retired, whose numbers had been growing both because of increasing longevity and the availability of government pensions that induced early retirement. In addition, along with other minorities, the retired had begun to assert their demands more vigorously in the sixties. Because social security benefits are widely regarded as having been paid for by the beneficiaries during their working years, the demands met little resistance. But in reality the benefits are a transfer from the current working population to the retired. The fiction becomes transparent only when the funding runs into problems. As long as the working population is much larger than the retired population and the benefits do not change, the tax consequences are bearable. Congress also was generous because nominally employers paid half the cost. Workers really carry part of that cost in the form of lower nominal wages and consumers bear the rest of it in the form of higher prices, but the fiction that employers pay the tax out of their profits persists. The social security tax on

Table 10.1

**GNP and Federal Nondefense Outlays in Billions of 1987 Dollars
and Indexes, 1970, 1980, 1987 (1970 = 100)**

	Billions of 1987 Dollars			Index Numbers		
	1970	1980	1987	1970	1980	1987
GNP	2,841.0	3,745.7	4,486.2	100	132	158
Total nondefense outlays	290.7	626.4	733.4	100	216	252
Social insurance[1]	111.6	231.2	297.5	100	207	267
Means-tested[2]	16.2	50.5	57.8	100	311	356
SSETE[3]	43.6	70.2	54.2	100	161	124
Education[4]	24.1	43.6	29.8	100	181	124
Community development	6.7	15.5	6.2	100	231	92
Agriculture	14.5	12.1	31.1	100	83	214
Veterans' benefits	24.3	29.1	26.7	100	119	110
Interest	40.3	72.0	137.5	100	179	341
Government[5]	19.9	29.8	29.7	100	150	150
Federal Retirement[6]	15.4	36.5	43.6	100	237	283
Other[7]	26.3	63.5	56.4	100	241	214

Sources: Statistical Abstract of the United States 1988, pp. 292–93, table 471; *Economic Report of the President 1988,* p. 248.

Note: Expenditures deflated by GNP implicit price deflator.

[1] Social Security, medicare, unemployment insurance.

[2] Housing assistance, food and nutrition assistance, other income security.

[3] General science, space and technology, environment, energy, transportation.

[4] Education, training, employment, and social services.

[5] International affairs, general government, administration of justice.

[6] Federal employee retirement and disability.

[7] Health, general retirement and disability insurance, general purpose fiscal assistance, commerce and housing credit.

employers also has the unfortunate effect of increasing the cost of labor and thus encouraging its substitution by machinery. The employer does not have to pay a social security tax on the use of machinery.

Congress had raised the pension benefits in two ways in the seventies. Earlier benefits had been based on a retiree's contributions while working, which were a percentage of average earnings over his or her working life. This average was usually less than the earnings at retirement owing to the rise in the general wage level, promotions, and seniority. The new formula allowed for this increase. In addition, the benefits were to rise each year with the cost of living. As a result, benefits rose rapidly. At the same time, however, workers' real earnings dropped slightly. Between 1970 and 1986 real average hourly compensation of employees in business sector production and nonsupervisory workers rose 12 percent,[1] while a retired couple's social security benefits increased by 50 percent.[2]

The image of the old as poor is no longer true: The fraction of the over–65 who are poor is smaller than among the young. Looking at cash income alone, the Bureau of the Census estimated that in 1985, 7 percent of families headed by someone over 65 were poor compared to 11.4 percent of all families.[3] Older people own more wealth than the young. More of them own their own homes and have paid off their mortgages. Thus, in 1984 households headed by an older person had a median net worth of $60,266 compared to $32,667 for all households.[4]

The administration and Congress did not dare to withdraw any of the benefits until the funds threatened to become exhausted. Current contributions were short of the payments in the early eighties owing to the recent inflation and the cost-of-living adjustment. Evading some of the responsibility, Reagan appointed the Greenspan Commission, which in 1983 recommended some changes, which Congress enacted. Scheduled increases in the social security tax were advanced to earlier dates. Benefits paid to families with incomes of over $32,000 became taxable, the receipts being credited to the social security system. The forecast is that the system will pay for itself until 2015.

Funds threaten to run out for medicare at the present growth rate of costs. General inflation, the rise in the cost of medical procedures, the larger number of beneficiaries, and the greater care given to each patient have contributed. The provision of medicare has itself been an element in the rise in the costs of medical care. The old now seek care for ailments that they would otherwise have ignored. In addition, medicare along with medical insurance has induced hospitals and physicians to provide more care for each ailment. Moreover, the growth in demand, in turn, has increased costs by raising the prices of services. The shift to fees set for diagnosis-related groups of illnessnes, regardless of the length of hospital stay or of the procedures used in each case, should give hospitals an incentive to economize.

The retired have exerted great political power. They were able to win a reduction in the share of physicians' fees that patients paid directly or through premiums for private insurance, and the deductible portion of hospital bills has not kept pace with the costs.

OTHER OUTLAYS

The heading "Means-tested payments" in Table 10.1 covers the various poverty programs. In the seventies, payments under Aid to Families with Dependent Children (AFDC) were increased, the older welfare programs for the blind, disabled, and elderly were combined under Supplemental Security Income (SSI), and food stamps came in 1970. The medicaid program was enacted in 1965. Costs increased as the participation of the eligible population grew and with inflation.

With other special interests well protected, the poor were left to suffer the crunch. The blacks' organizations were their only lobby, and the poor did not vote. Needless to say, the middle class was far more numerous and voted. Not only did the Republicans gain the White House as a result, but among Democrats the liberals lost influence, and most supported a larger defense effort and lower taxes.

Not surprisingly, the Reagan budget for 1982 cut the payments for the politically vulnerable poverty programs. The eligibility rules for means-tested payments were tightened so that only the "truly poor" were helped. The change reduced the percentage of poor children whose families received payments to 55 in 1984; it had been as high as 79 percent.[5] In addition, many of the working poor were excluded from the programs, raising the incentive to drop out of the labor force. In addition, AFDC payments did not keep up with inflation. In real terms payment per recipient in 1986 was 14 percent less than in 1970.[6] The administration also cut matching funds for medicaid.

Summing up, between 1980 and 1987 the means-tested payments grew only 15 percent in constant dollars, and much of the growth was due to the rapid rise of medicaid costs. Another element was the persistence of a high rate of unemployment among unskilled workers. The average unemployment rate for machine operators, assemblers, and inspectors in 1987 was 8.9 percent and for handlers, equipment cleaners, helpers, and laborers it was 12.4 percent.[7]

Farmers won much bigger gains in assistance. In 1987 farm subsidies were more than two and one-half times as large in real terms as in 1980. Government subsidies became a major source of farmers' income. The share of the GNP originating in agriculture contributed by these payments amounted to as much as 41 percent in 1986.[8] The payments amounted to no less than $11,000 per person employed in agriculture.[9]

The improvement in agricultural methods in other countries, with the help of U.S. agricultural experts, did not do our farmers much good. The resulting large crops depressed the prices of grains. Nor did the rise of the dollar help. The farmers were especially vulnerable after the good markets of the seventies had induced them to go into debt to buy land. The government programs continue to maintain the U.S. prices of wheat, cotton, rice, corn, tobacco, and sugar at high levels in the face of falling world prices. The usual justification is that uncontrollable weather and other conditions cause price instability. But U.S. agriculture is not undergoing a temporary drop in demand. Productivity in Africa, China, and India has improved, and India now can export food.

Furthermore, European farmers also are being supported by their governments. These programs in various countries create a perverse incentive to produce more in the face of falling prices. Despite these recognized effects, the governments continue their policies. These are not stabilization programs. The governments are subsidizing agriculture despite the accumulating surpluses.

NASA, other research enterprises, and pollution control have suffered from the budgetary crunch. The drop in oil prices in 1983

Table 10.2

Estimates of Possible Savings in Nondefense Programs in 1988

	Savings ($ billions)
Reduce medicare benefits and increase fees for services	6.1
Limit cost-of-living adjustments in social security benefits	5.8
Reduce veterans' disability benefits	2.2
Require two-week wait for unemployment insurance payments	0.9
Terminate general revenue sharing	4.6
Reduce agricultural price supports	2.5
Phase out public works programs	3.3
Reduce energy cost support	2.5
Eliminate business subsidies	2.9
Scale back nondefense construction	1.6
Recover costs of regulation	3.0
Reduce subsidies for transportation	6.4
Reduce subsidies for sewage treatment, power, export-import bank, postal service	1.6
Reduce poverty programs, including legal services, housing, Urban Development Action grants, Economic Development Administration, and Community Development Block grants	3.5
Reduce expenditures for education and training	1.4
Reduce veterans' health services	1.3
Reduce civil service employee benefits	4.6
Total	54.2

Source: Based on Congress of the United States, Congressional Budget Office, *Reducing the Deficit: Spending and Revenue Options.* A Report to the Senate and House Committees on the Budget—Part II, March 1986, pp. 77–218.

made energy a less pressing problem, resulting in a drop in expenditures. On the other hand, Amtrak, the airlines, and shipping continue to be subsidized. Expenditures for community programs, job training, Head Start, and for education have been slashed, as have payments under revenue sharing to the state and local governments. The continued high deficit, together with high interest rates have more than doubled interest payments since 1980.

FURTHER CUTS IN EXPENDITURES

The Congressional Budget Office (CBO) has proposed a list of politically possible expenditure cuts. These are set out in broad categories in Table 10.2.

The total nondefense cuts deemed possible by the CBO add up to $54.2 billion. If we add these to the $15 billion sum of defense cuts that the CBO also judged possible, it makes a total of $69.2 billion. This is still a long way from $150 billion.

Other cuts apparently would be much more difficult. The CBO judged that the cost-of-living adjustment in social security benefits might be reduced, but Congress could not resist the opposition to any additional reductions. The farmers' lobby evidently is so powerful that the CBO could not see Congress making a deep slash in their subsidies.

Indeed, the CBO understated the difficulty of making any significant dent in nondefense expenditures by not considering demands that are not being met. Prisons will become even more overcrowded without more funds. Elementary and secondary education are paid for locally, but a significant improvement may require larger federal expenditures. Pollution has worsened.

The president is unlikely to have more than a marginal effect on total expenditures. None of the Democratic candidates for the presidential nomination made defense a major issue, to say nothing of the Republican candidates. President Bush is unlikely to recommend the major changes in defense policy required for a substantial reduction in expenditures. Social security, medicare, veterans' benefits, and the retirement benefits of federal employees remain sacrosanct. Interest must continue to be paid. Expenditures for the poor, science, space, highways, agriculture, education, the prisons, and the ordinary business of government could not possibly provide the economies needed to eliminate the deficit.

11
PROPOSALS

REDUCE THE BUDGET DEFICIT

Peterson and Rohatyn have exaggerated the effects of the budget deficit on the interest rate and through the interest rate on the dollar, exports and imports, and employment in manufacturing. The Fed's tight monetary policy, the decline in velocity, and the growth of demand for credit by the private sector did more to raise the interest rate than the deficit. Even at its peak the deficit had a smaller influence than Peterson and Rohatyn have argued. Now that the deficit is down to 3.1 percent of the GNP, its influence is neglible.

Moreover, how can Peterson and Rohatyn condemn the deficit unless they judge that it has raised the real interest rate to an excessive height? It is, of course, higher than in the seventies. But the lender-robbing negative real interest rate of the period of high inflation is not a good standard. The current (December 1988) inflation rate is about 4.5 percent, and the nominal rate on 10-year Treasury bonds is about 9.1 percent. Subtracting the inflation rate from the nominal interest rate gives us a real rate of 4.6 percent. Historically this is high. However, business activity and therefore the demand for credit remain high. In addition, as we have seen, we can no longer decide whether or not the rate of interest in the United States is high or low without looking at other countries. The United States is part of the world money market. The U.S. real rate is no higher than it is in Japan or in West Germany. In

Japan, where the inflation rate is zero, the nominal and therefore the real rate of interest on 10-year government bonds is 5.2 percent. In West Germany, where 10-year government bonds yield 6.8 percent and the rate of inflation is less than 1 percent, the real rate is above 5.8 percent.[1]

Since the U.S. real interest rate is less than that of Japan or West Germany, it is not raising the exchange rates for the dollar. Moreover, the exchange rates probably are below purchasing power parity rates—the rates that would prevail were they determined only by the demand for the dollar for imports and exports. According to Ronald I. McKinnon of Stanford University, the dollar has been below its purchasing power parity with the yen and the mark since mid–1986.[2] The exchange rates for the dollar are no longer high.

The continuing trade deficit thus is not due to high exchange rates. The general prosperity is responsible for the excess of imports over exports, not high exchange rates. As long as the boom continues, imports will remain large, and when U.S. manufacturers are straining capacity limits they cannot expand their exports much more.

Nevertheless, the goal should be to reduce the budget deficit. This should be the goal, not because either the interest rate or the trade deficit is excessive, but because we do not want the public debt to keep mounting. Since the growth rate of the public debt is higher than the growth rate of total output, to maintain the deficit at its present percentage of the GNP may impose a heavy burden on posterity. The government need not go to the length of setting the objective of a zero deficit, as it did by passing the Gramm-Rudman-Hollings amendment. Complete elimination is unreasonable and unnecessary. Investment expenditures by the government, which add to the economy's productivity, warrant a deficit. The faster the GNP grows, the smaller is the debt burden. Since federal investment expenditures may equal or exceed the present deficit, the long-run burden may not grow even if we maintain the present deficit as a percentage of the GNP. Nevertheless, since public investments probably do not match private investments in productivity, the deficit should be cut.

In addition, we have to worry about retaining some flexibility in fiscal policy to cope with recessions, as well as about the future

burden of the debt. The current, long prosperity has n̶
recessions a thing of the past. The federal budget will show u̶c̶..̶
at such times, regardless of the administration's and Congress's
intentions. Moreover, during a recession the administration may
want to promote full employment by increasing public expenditures to above the level of the preceding prosperous period or by
reducing taxes. To permit such antirecession, stimulative policies
without accumulating a large public debt in the process, the deficit
should be small during prosperous periods, including the present
one. A more reasonable objective than the one imposed by the
Gramm-Rudman-Hollings amendment is to set the deficit limit at
1 percent of the GNP during periods of prosperity. At the current
level of the GNP, the limit would be about $50 billion—about one-
third of the current level of $150 billion. A later section discusses
how this objective should be achieved.

RESTRAIN THE FED

The Fed should be restrained from manipulating the money supply as freely as it has in the past. Its expansionist policies brought
on the high inflation rate of the late seventies, and its restrictive
policies brought on recessions in 1970, 1974, and a particularly
severe one in 1982. Its restrictive policy in 1980 and 1981 helped
raise the dollar, causing a large negative trade balance. The Fed's
restrictiveness in 1987 brought about the stock market crash. The
Fed has performed badly as a forecaster and as an agency for stabilizing the economy.

The Fed cannot expect to perform well as an active regulator of
the money market. The assumption that money managers and
bankers are automatons reacting mechanically to movements in
interest rates without attempting to make forecasts of their own is
wrong. If money managers act on their own forecasts, then the
Fed cannot hope to achieve its chief objective of stabilizing prices.

If the Fed wants to prevent inflation, it raises the interest rate by
reducing the stock of money. The theory is that unrestrained, a
rising level of business activity feeds inflationary expectations that
are self-fulfilling. However, if sellers, buyers, and the Fed expect
inflation, then so, too, do lenders. The interest rate will already
have risen in anticipation of inflation. Lenders watch the real interest

rate, not the nominal one. True, lenders accepted low rates in the seventies, even negative rates. They did not expect prices to rise as rapidly as they did. But they will not repeat that mistake. Lenders have learned to beware of inflation. For the Fed to step in and raise the interest rate when lenders already anticipate inflation may lead to an excessively high and destabilizing interest rate. Further, if the lenders expect the Fed's intervention during periods of threatening inflation, then they are more likely to overshoot and demand an even higher interest rate than they would otherwise. With inflation or recession threatening, Congress, the administration, the media, and members of the financial community press the Fed to not just sit there but to do something, and the Fed itself wants activity, if for no other reason than to justify its existence. Congress did not create the Fed simply to watch the economy. It expects the Fed to control interest rates and the price level and to prevent recessions. But an active Fed does not assure greater stability. The record reveals the opposite to be true: An active Fed adds to the instability.

The Fed should give up attempting to regulate interest rates, the dollar, and the inflation rate. Instead, it should limit itself to adding to the stock of money at a constant rate, regardless of what the economy is doing at the moment. The goal of zero inflation would dictate a growth rate of the money supply equal to the average growth rate of real GNP over some extended period—perhaps the last five years. As we saw earlier, the average growth rate of real GNP since 1980 has been 2.6 percent. The growth rate of M2 generally has been much higher. In recent years the rate usually has exceeded 8 percent. To bring the money supply growth rate down to 3 percent or less would bring down inflation, but it would also bring about a recession. Too many contracts have been written in anticipation of the current rate of inflation. As we have seen, a slowing down in the growth rate of the money supply has reduced output more than prices. In the immediate future, therefore, the Fed should keep the money supply growing at the rate of 8 percent.

However, over time the Fed should reduce the growth rate. A zero inflation rate should be the ultimate objective, since the impact even of the current apparently tolerable inflation rate is uneven. Some prices are more rigid than others. In New York rents are controlled, and landlords have failed to win increases that compensate for inflation, resulting in a deteriorating housing stock.

Welfare recipients have not kept up with inflation. Interest rates adjust slowly, so pensioners living on earnings from bonds and mortgages suffer from inflation. To bring the inflation rate down to zero the Fed will have to slow down the growth of the money supply gradually to the rate of growth of the real GNP.

The president can influence the Fed's policies through his power to appoint the chairman and the members of its Board of Governors. Moreover, a determined president can stop the Fed's dangerous activism through appointments and open appeals. Past presidents have wanted an active Fed, and they have succeeded in getting one. Carter appointed William Miller as chairman because he wanted easier credit. Miller carried through, with disastrous results. It is time that the Fed was instructed to refrain from exercising its huge power to disrupt the economy.

NO INDUSTRIAL POLICY

An industrial policy is unnecessary. During the eighties U.S. manufacturing has performed very well. Output has grown rapidly, despite the rise of the dollar. Manufacturing generally has improved its efficiency and labor productivity. The resulting reductions in costs have enabled manufacturers to retain their markets. U.S. manufacturing industries' gains in productivity compare favorably with those of most Western industrialized countries.

The fall in manufacturing employment has been due to the productivity gains, not to loss of markets as proponents of an industrial policy say. Output has grown faster than the labor force. The gains in productivity have enabled manufacturers to produce a larger volume of goods with fewer employees. It also needs saying that part of the nominal loss of employment reflects an increase in the average number of hours worked per employee.

In international comparisons, the United States comes out pretty well. U.S. manufacturers did not perform as well as Japanese manufacturers. The Japanese did better both in output growth and in productivity growth. However, U.S. manufacturers did better than those of other OECD countries in output growth, and better than most of them in productivity growth.

An industrial policy is not only unnecessary, but it is likely to do harm. An industrial policy will be the excuse for measures to subsidize and protect declining U.S. manufacturing industries, such as leather, apparel, and steel. The policy will impose higher costs on consumers, and it will rob manufacturers of their incentive to improve productivity. The agencies charged with responsibility will look after producers' interests, not those of consumers.

The United States should maintain its present policy of trade liberalization. The rise of the dollar, not the reduction in tariffs, caused the excessive growth of the trade imbalance. The continuing trade imbalance is due to the slowness with which exporters and importers adjust to the lower dollar and to the long prosperity. Another important element is the higher level of business activity in the United States than in other countries. The reduction in tariffs brought about by the Kennedy round of trade negotiations under GATT succeeded in raising both exports and imports to the United States. Moreover, the growth of imports and the loss of exports during the eighties, which was due principally to the high value of the dollar, induced manufacturers to improve their efficiency and thus their competitive position in world markets. The lower tariff barriers added to the inducement.

The industries in which the United States performs well are those that employ skilled workers. These do not need protection against foreign competition, and raising tariffs to protect declining industries, which employ less skilled workers, will reduce the exports of the growing industries and thus total exports by inviting retaliation by other countries. The high-performance industries are principally the machinery industries, both electrical and nonelectrical. U.S. manufacturers of computers, components of computers, and of office machinery generally have done especially well. During the eighties their growth has been phenomenal. It is unlikely that an industrial policy would promote the growth of these industries. It is more likely to do damage. An industrial policy may protect the declining industries, but only at a high cost to consumers and to the detriment of the growing industries.

Currently assistance is provided to workers who are displaced by the growth of imports under trade adjustment assistance programs. Benefits under these programs have been less generous than was anticipated at the outset. These may be increased, and the rules for eligibility may be liberalized.

PUBLIC EXPENDITURES

State and local government services should be given a higher priority than in recent years. In coming years, expenditures for education, highways, police, and sanitation services will have to increase. State and local governments also will have to raise their tax rates to pay the costs of meeting national pollution standards.

The state and local governments should raise the bulk of their revenues through their own taxes and not depend on the federal government. They should pay for their own services. A rich locality, which wants daily garbage collections, good protection against fire and theft, and well-equipped schools employing good teachers, should pay the costs. Formulas for distributing federal assistance cannot be finely attuned to the varying needs and capabilities of raising revenues across localities.

Chapter 7 argues that taxpayers have accepted reductions in the quality of state and local government services because the costs of matching the quality of the fifties have risen enormously. This is true for education and for police, fire, sanitation, and public hospital services. The prices of these services relative to the prices of manufactured goods are much higher now than they were in the fifties. This does not imply that the federal government should undertake to pay the costs of state and local services. However, the federal tax system should leave room for state and local governments to raise their own taxes. The federal government should continue to allow state and local taxes to be deducted from gross income in calculating the federal personal income tax. Allowing these deductions partly contravenes the principle that local consumers of services should pay for them. However, without such deductions the quality of some services is likely to deteriorate to unacceptable levels in many communities. There is a national interest in preserving some minimum level of quality in police and other services throughout the country. In addition, the federal government should not invade the field of sales taxes, a major source of state and local revenue.

A good beginning to bringing up state and local government services to a more acceptable quality level would be for the federal government to give as much assistance to these governments in constant dollars as it did in 1980. To restore the assistance to the earlier level would require additional expenditures of $10 billion.

Highways present a special problem, since the interstates serve both national and local needs. The condition of many of the roads and bridges has deteriorated because of lack of maintenance. In some cases the conditions are unacceptable, even dangerous. The costs of restoring roads and bridges will have to be divided among the various governments. Since the federal government has easier access to funds, it will have to carry the major share. Again, federal expenditures for highways in 1980 were much higher than in 1987. A return to the level of 1980 would require $7 billion in additional expenditures. The Bush administration should propose additional appropriations of this magnitude.

The case cannot be denied that the federal government should contribute to the costs of education in poor communities because the burden of supporting a class of unskilled unemployables ultimately falls on the nation as a whole. Nevertheless, the basic responsibility should remain where it is. The federal government should pay more of the costs of education in low-income areas, but in general localities should bear most of the costs.

To restore federal expenditures for primary, secondary, and higher education to their levels in 1980 would require additional expenditures of $8 billion at 1988 prices. It is proposed that expenditures be raised by $10 billion and that the additional money be spent entirely on primary and secondary school education.

The federal government should increase expenditures for public aid. Poverty has not been a local problem for a long time. Much of the burdens now carried by the large cities reflect widespread economic problems originating elsewhere. The migration of southern rural workers displaced by agricultural productivity improvements imposed a huge welfare problem on the cities. Similarly, unemployment resulting from recessions, from gains in manufacturing productivity, or from foreign competition should not impose large costs on the localities in which particular industries are concentrated. Although public welfare programs necessarily are locally administered, their financing by local governments, which reflects the problems of an earlier period when each locality looked after its own poor, is inappropriate today. Finally, states and localities compete for new taxpaying residents and businesses by promising low tax rates. The competition deprives them of the funds to pay for necessary services and more particularly for assistance to the poor.

For the federal government to restore the 1980 level of its expenditures for poverty assistance would require an additional $4 billion.

The costs of medicare and of medicaid will grow with the aging of the population and the continued advances in medical technology, which tend to be expensive. It is difficult to refuse organ transplants to patients, however old they are and however expensive the procedure is. The federal government also is likely to bear more of the costs of catastrophic illnesses than it does now. The burden of carrying the costs of nursing the chronically ill looms. The Bush administration should plan to spend $10 billion more than is currently being spent for medicare. Medicaid will probably require $4 billion more.

The Reagan administration cut expenditures for the environment. Toxic wastes remain as serious a problem as they were a decade ago, despite efforts by the various governments to reduce the problem. Air and water quality problems also are a long way from being solved. Additional expenditures of $10 billion are proposed for this purpose.

Not all the items requiring additional expenditures have been listed. These include public housing and training programs for the jobless. In addition, higher interest rates and the continuing rise in the public debt will require increases in interest payments. Moreover, some of the estimates of funds needed for the items that have been mentioned may be low. An allowance of $10 billion is proposed.

The total of proposed additional expenditures comes to $65 billion. In addition, $100 billion will be needed to reduce the deficit to 1 percent of the GNP.

A large part of the funds needed can come out of those now spent on defense. Chapter 9 argues that the current high defense expenditures are based on an excessive assessment of the Soviet threat. Even though eliminating expenditures for new strategic weapons and for SDI research will save only a small fraction of total defense expenditures, they should be stopped. The deployment of strategic weapons increases the risk that a preemptive attack will set off a nuclear war. This risk is much greater than that of a deliberate Soviet attack, which strategic weapons are intended to deter. The administration should not have any additional MX missiles deployed and should remove those already deployed. Nor should it deploy any Trident IIs. These weapons increase the risk of a preemptive attack by threatening a first strike. The deployment of strategic defense weapons also will enhance the danger of nuclear warfare. We should retain that retaliatory capability that does not pose the risk of a U.S. first strike to the Soviet Union.

Radical as it may appear to be, the proposed change will not require a fundamental shift in defense policy. Neither the Reagan administration nor any of its predecessors seriously contemplated the use of strategic weapons other than for retaliation against a nuclear attack. The U.S. defense policy has been aimed at the deterrence of a deliberate Soviet nuclear attack. A secondary objective, but one that was far from clearly delineated, was to deter a conventional attack against Western Europe. The vague hope was that the Soviets would refrain from launching their conventional forces, despite their alleged superiority over NATO's, out of fear of triggering an attack by superior U.S. strategic forces. Without superiority in strategic weapons, the deterrent against a conventional attack would be either ineffective or at any rate less effective. The thinking was not clear. It is even less clear today. This is why no fundamental change will be required by a decision not to deploy new strategic weapons. That decision only requires a clearer conception of the purposes of our current defense policy. The current force of SLBMs and Minuteman IIIs effectively deter any Soviet nuclear attack. The Soviets will not risk their own nuclear destruction for any conceivable military gains that might result from a nuclear attack or the threat of one, however superior their own forces may be. This is why Reagan was willing to discuss with Gorbachev at Reykjavik the complete dismantling of nuclear defenses by both countries. The continuing thaw in U.S.-Soviet relations since that summit meeting has brought us even closer to the point where we feel that strategic superiority is not necessary for security.

The suggested reductions in the strategic forces alone will not save enough money to pay for the proposed additions to nondefense expenditures. Even the complete elimination of expenditures for strategic forces would save only a small fraction of total defense expenditures. Safety is the primary goal, not economies.

Large economies would require a fundamental change in defense policy. To reduce expenditures by half to about 3.2 percent from the current 6.4 percent of the GNP would require a large reduction in the size of the conventional forces. Such savings in defense would make adequate funds available for the nation's state and local government services, medicare, medicaid, and other programs mentioned earlier. The United States could not cut its defense expenditures by half without substantially reducing the size of its conventional forces. To achieve such economies, the United States would have to withdraw its forces from Western Europe and South Korea and abandon the maritime strategy.

National security would not be threatened by the withdrawal of forces from Western Europe. Western Europe spends a smaller percentage of its GNP on defense than the United States does, and for some time now it has been rich enough to support adequate conventional forces without U.S. assistance to deter a Soviet attack. NATO's conventional forces now are strong enough to deter a Soviet attack. The American commitment was made under the delusion of a strongly expansionist Soviet dictatorship, which was willing to risk the destruction of its country to achieve imperialist goals, in particular the conquest of Western Europe. The United States also exaggerated Soviet military strength. Recent reassessments are much more optimistic. Gorbachev's major goal is to raise the Soviet standard of living, not to build up resources for an attack on the West. The CIA's newest estimates of Soviet defense expenditures reveal a much slower rate of growth than its earlier estimates.

Reports of resistance to Gorbachev's attempts to reform the Soviet economic and political system argue for the West's retention of a strong defense system. We cannot hang all our security on Gorbachev's remaining in power. But even if Soviet bureaucrats remove Gorbachev, any successor is unlikely to take great risks, as our defense policy assumes. Since military strategists are uncertain about the outcome of a conventional war, Soviet forces invading Western Europe will not gain an easy victory. The Soviets are unlikely to undertake a costly war. Nor are the Soviets likely to risk a nuclear war by undertaking a major conventional war. As long as each side can inflict nuclear destruction on the other, a major war entails the risk of a nuclear attack. If the Soviets overrun Western Europe with their conventional forces, the United States may try to force them back with the threat of a nuclear attack.

Western Europe can make up for the withdrawal of American forces without undue sacrifice. NATO's defenses could be improved without major new expenditures through the integration of the French forces with those of NATO. Because the French forces are not part of NATO's forces, they do not train together. Moreover, at the outbreak of a war, the French forces will not be immediately involved. Complete integration would strengthen the defenses considerably.

In addition, the United States does not supply a large part of NATO's defenses. Of the total NATO strength, including the French, the United States supplies 14 percent. It supplies a larger part of the total expenditures. But Western Europe also can make up for the loss of the U.S. contribution without undue sacrifice. Other members of NATO spend a much smaller percentage of their GNP on defense than does the United States.

Finally, Western Europe has a large population and it is wealthier than the Soviet Union. It should be able to mount sufficiently strong defenses to deter a Soviet attack.

From time to time the United States has considered withdrawing its troops from South Korea. That country can defend itself against an attack by North Korea without U.S. assistance. It is richer than North Korea and it can easily match the potential enemy's strength. South Korea does not have as large forces, but it can add to them. The U.S. presence, which is a hangover from the Korean War, is no longer necessary.

The expensive maritime strategy has the hopeless and dangerous objective of destroying the Soviet nuclear submarines at their base at the outset of a war. Not only will its abandonment result in large savings, but it will reduce the risk of a conventional war becoming a nuclear war.

The adoption of these proposals will require a fundamental change in defense policy, which will not take place without a major national debate. Despite the recent arms control agreement, the continuing negotiations over reductions in long-range nuclear weapons, and the current détente, the United States is not ready to reduce its defense expenditures substantially. The Soviet bogey retains much of its power.

Nevertheless, a continuing détente may encourage the Bush administration and Congress to make substantial reductions in defense expenditures. Abandonment of the maritime strategy probably requires less of a fundamental change than would withdrawal from NATO, and we may be nearly ready to give it up. Military strategists, who support a strong defense, have doubted the feasilibility of the plan for a massive attack on the Soviet SLBM base. In addition, the vulnerability of the carriers to guided missiles remains in question. Moreover, some recent reductions in proposed outlays for ships suggest that the Defense Department will not continue to press for a 15-carrier navy.

By itself, a withdrawal from South Korea is no drastic change. The proposal is not new; past administrations have contemplated carrying it out. Nevertheless, it may be difficult for the Bush administration to propose the withdrawal as part of a general reduction in conventional strength.

The big change would be the withdrawal from NATO. Our national policy has assumed for too long that when the Soviets expect to gain a victory in Western Europe they will invade, for us to be able to quit NATO without a wrenching debate. Ever since World War II no candidate for the presidency has dared propose the abandonment of NATO, the centerpiece of our defense policy.

This book proposes halving our defense expenditures because it is the sensible way to raise the funds needed for other purposes, not because of any optimism that the Bush administration and Congress are ready to go ahead.

We may not be able to reduce defense expenditures by 3.2 percent of GNP, but it should be possible to reduce them by 1.4 to 5 percent without great political travail. This would be just under the level reached in 1980 under Carter. To bring defense expenditures down to that level would require a cut of $70 billion. The estimated total of procurement expenditures is about $80 billion.[3] Of this total, approximately $9 billion is for missiles, including strategic and other nuclear weapons. In addition, the Defense Department asked for $2.7 billion for ballistic missiles. Another $9 billion is for new ships, including $1.4 billion for a Trident ballistic missile submarine and $3.1 billion for three attack submarines. Proposed procurement expenditures also include $17.4 billion for new aircraft, including an undisclosed amount for the Stealth bomber, whose mission is to follow up an initial strategic missile attack and destroy surviving Soviet targets. Other procurement expenditures are for support equipment, vehicles including tanks and Bradley troop carriers, communications equipment, and ammunition. It should be possible to reduce the procurement expenditures by $28 billion to $52 billion in 1989 dollars. This would be the same level as in 1980.[4]

Proposed research, development, test, and evaluation (RDT&E) funding comes to $38.2 billion.[5] Of this total, $4.5 billion is for the Strategic Defense Initiative (SDI). Cutting RDT&E expenditures back to the 1980 level in 1989 dollars would save $18.5 billion.[6]

Of the total proposed reduction of $70 billion, $23.5 billion remain to be allocated. Further cuts may be made on closer study in the procurement and RDT&E accounts. Alternatively, expenditures for military personnel and operations and maintenance (O&M) may be cut by this amount. In constant dollars, expenditures for military personnel in 1989 will exceed those of 1980 by $26 billion, and the difference for O&M will be approximately $16 billion.[7] It should be possible to cut total expenditures by an additional $23.5 billion without great difficulty.

Agricultural subsidies have mounted during the Reagan years. Reducing them to the 1980 level can provide another source of funds. It is proposed that these expenditures be reduced by $15 billion.

Thus, of the total $165 billion required for reducing the deficit plus new expenditures, defense and agricultural subsidies can provide $85 billion. An additional $80 billion will be required. If GNP continues to grow at the average rate of the eighties, revenues will grow by $26 billion without new taxes or increases in tax rates.

The residual reduction of $59 billion will require new tax revenues. To raise these additional revenues entirely through the personal income tax would add about 4 percentage points to the present tax rates across the board. This would impose a heavy burden on lower-income families. An attempt to apply the principle of progressive taxation and raise the new revenue entirely from higher-income groups would raise the rates at the upper end greatly.

New tax sources will be needed. One possibility is the value-added tax (VAT) discussed in Chapter 8. A 1 percent VAT, with housing, food, and medical expenses exempt, would raise a substantial part of the needed funds. An alternative would be a gasoline tax. An increase of 2 percentage points in the personal income tax rates for incomes over $30,000 combined with a 1 percent VAT should provide sufficient revenues. Limiting the increase in personal income taxes in this way would conform to the progressiveness principle. A VAT with the specified exemptions would also conform to the principle. Stricter adherence to the principle would prohibit either a VAT or a gasoline tax and require a larger and more progressive rise in the personal income tax rates. A larger increase in the personal income tax rates across the board would reduce the supply of labor, particularly that of married women. The advantage of consumption taxes, such as a VAT or a gasoline tax, is that they do not reduce work incentives.

A steeper schedule of rates would spur Congress to introduce deductions from taxable income to encourage socially desirable behavior. Proposals have been made recently to encourage college education by allowing part of the associated expenses to be deducted from taxable income. Such changes would soon bring us back to a tax system riddled with favors for particular groups.

NOTES

CHAPTER 1

1. Peter Peterson, *The Atlantic Monthly*, October 1987.
2. Felix Rohatyn, "What Next?" *The New York Review of Books*, December 3, 1987, pp. 3–5.
3. Lester C. Thurow, *The Zero-Sum Solution: Building a World-Class American Economy* (New York: Simon & Schuster, 1985).
4. Robert Reich, *The Next American Frontier* (New York: New York Times Books, 1983).
5. The Cuomo Commission on Trade and Competitiveness, *The Cuomo Commission Report: A New American Formula for a Strong Economy* (New York: Simon & Schuster, 1988).

CHAPTER 2

1. *Economic Report of the President 1988* (Washington D.C.: U.S. GPO, 1988), p. 337, table B–76.
2. Ibid., p. 251, Table B–2.
3. Robert Eisner, *How Real Is the Federal Deficit?* (New York: The Free Press, 1986).
4. Ibid., p. 31.

CHAPTER 3

1. A W H. Phillips, "The Relation between Unemployment and the Rate of Change of Money Wage Rates in the United Kingdom, 1861–1957," *Economica* (November 1958): 283–99.
2. OLS regression equations for 1968–1987 are as follows:

$$p_t = 7.80 - 0.17m_{t-1} \qquad \overline{R}^2 = .04$$
$$(t = -0.85)$$

$$g_t = 3.57 + 0.67m_{t-1} \qquad \overline{R}^2 = .47$$
$$(t = 4.13)$$

p_t = percent growth of GNP deflator in year t from year $t-1$
g_t = percent increase in constant-dollar GNP in year t from year $t-1$.
m_{t-1} = percent growth of M2 in year $t-1$ from year $t-2$.

CHAPTER 4

1. Robert Reich, *The Next American Frontier* (New York: New York Times Books, 1983).
2. Lester Thurow, *The Zero-Sum Solution: Building a World-Class American Economy* (New York: Simon & Schuster, 1985).

CHAPTER 5

1. *Federal Reserve Bulletin*, November 1987, p. A3; ibid., February 1988, p. A3.

CHAPTER 6

1. Bureau of Labor Statistics.
2. Bureau of Labor Statistics.
3. Bureau of Labor Statistics.
4. *Statistical Abstract of the United States 1988*, table 640, p. 385.
5. Ibid., p. 391, table 645.
6. U S. Supreme Court, No. 83–2004.
7. Bureau of Labor Statistics, press release July 6, 1988.
8. *Economic Report of the President 1988*, p. 284, table B–32.
9. *Economic Report of the President 1988*, p. 261, table B–11.
10. Bureau of Labor Statistics, July 6, 1988.

11. Ibid.

12. Ibid.

13. Based on *Statistical Abstract of the United States 1988*, p. 508, table 849.

14. Based on *Economic Report of the President 1988*, p. 300, table B–46; Moody's AAA corporate bond rate deflated by consumer price index, ibid., p. 330, table B–71, and ibid., p. 313, table B–58.

15. *Statistical Abstract of the United States 1977*, p. 793, table 1360; *Statistical Abstract of the United States 1988*, p. 701, table 1241.

16. *The Economic Report of the President 1988*, p. 286, table B–33 indicates that total employment grew at the rate of 1.8 percent per year. For manufacturing employment to have remained at the same percentage of total employment, it would have had to grow at the same rate, or 1 percentage point more than it did. Assuming that productivity growth would have been unaffected, total output would have had to rise 1 percentage point more than it did.

17. Based on *Economic Report of the President 1988*, p. 300, table B–46.

18. *Statistical Abstract of the United States 1988*, p. 391, table 644.

19. Based on Bureau of Labor Statistics, press release July 6, 1988.

20. Ibid.

21. Ibid.

22. Ibid.

CHAPTER 7

1. *Statistical Abstract of the United States 1988*, p. 158, table 283, *Historical Statistics* vol. 1, p. 413, series H952.

2. *Statistical Abstract of the United States 1988*, p. 175, table 305.

3. Based on ibid., p. 446, table 733, and *Historical Statistics*, vol. 1, p. 198, series E1–22.

4. *Economic Report of the President 1988*, p. 279.

5. Ibid., pp. 252, 342. Federal, state, and local government transfer payments deflated by GNP implicit deflator.

6. Expenditures in current dollars from Office of the Assistant Secretary of Defense (Comptroller), *National Defense Budget Estimates for FY1988/1989*, April 1988, pp. 64, 66. Deflated by GNP implicit price deflator, *Economic Report of the President 1988*, p. 252.

7. *Statistical Abstract of the United States 1988*, p. 258; *Historical Statistics*, pp. 1120–21, series Y533–566. Deflated by GNP implicit deflator for state and local government purchases of goods and services, *Economic Report of the President 1988*, p. 253.

8. *Statistical Abstract of the United States 1988*, p. 126, table 204.

9. Ibid., p. 262, Table 437.
10. Ibid., p. 260, Table 434.

CHAPTER 8

1. *Economic Report of the President 1988*, p. 337, table B–76.
2. Edward F. Denison, *Trends in American Economic Growth, 1929–1982*, (Washington, D.C.: The Brookings Institution, 1985), p. 111.
3. Joseph A. Pechman, "Tax Reform: Theory and Practice," *Economic Perspectives*, 1, 1 (*summer* 1987): 19.
4. David Stockman, *The Triumph of Politics* (New York: Avon, 1987).

CHAPTER 9

1. David Schwartzman, *Games of Chicken: Four Decades of the American Nuclear Defense Policy* (New York: Praeger, 1988).
2. Based on Schwartzman, *Games of Chicken.*
3. Adam B. Ulam, *The Rivals: America and Russia Since World War II* (New York: Penguin, 1971); Thomas W. Wolfe, *Soviet Power and Europe, 1945–1970* (Baltimore: Johns Hopkins Univ. Press, 1970); Joseph L. Nogee and Robert H. Donaldson, *Soviet Foreign Policy Since World War II* (New York: Pergamon, 1981); David Holloway, *The Soviet Union and the Arms Race* (New Haven, CT: Yale Univ. Press, 1983); Robin Edmonds, *Soviet Foreign Policy: The Brezhnev Years* (Oxford: Oxford University Press, 1983); Marshall D. Shulman, "Relations with the Soviet Union," in Kermit Gordon, ed. *Agenda for the Nation: Papers on Domestic and Foreign Policy Issues* (Washington, D.C.: Brookings Institution, 1968), pp. 373–406.
4. Joshua M. Epstein, *The 1987 Defense Budget* (Washington, D.C.: The Brookings Institution, 1986), pp. 28–40.
5. Richard F. Kaufman, "Causes of the Slowdown in Soviet Defense," *Soviet Economy* 1, 1 (*1985*): 9–12.
6. *Report of the Secretary of Defense Caspar Weinberger to the Congress on the FY 1985 Budget*, p. 20.
7. Based on William M. Kaufmann, *A Reasonable Defense* (Washington, D.C.: The Brookings Institution, 1986), p. 14.
8. Estimated on basis of *SAUS 1988*, p. 315, tables 511 and 512. Includes R&D expenditures plus expenditures for atomic energy defense activities in Department of Energy.
9. David Stockman, *The Triumph of Politics: The Inside Story of the Reagan Revolution* (New York: Avon, 1987) pp. 116–19.
10. Ibid., pp. 304–5.

11. Office of the Assistant Secretary of Defense (Comptroller), *National Defense Budget Estimates for FY 1988/1989*, May 1987, table 6.7, p. 87.

12. Ibid., table 3.4, p. 24, table 6.6, p. 88.

13. Joshua M. Epstein, *The 1987 Defense Budget* (Washington, D.C.: Brookings Institution, 1986), pp. 41–42.

14. Office of the Assistant Secretary of Defense (Comptroller), *National Defense Budget Estimates for FY 1988/1989*, April 1988, p. 23, table 3.4.

15. Congressional Budget Office (CBO), *Modernizing U.S. Strategic Offensive Forces: The Administration's Program and Alternatives* (Washington, D.C.: U.S. GPO, May 1983,) p. 24.

16. Ibid., p. 3.

17. Ibid., p. 46.

18. CBO, *Trident II Missiles: Capability, Costs, and Alternatives* (Washington, D.C.: Government Printing Office, 1986), p. 26. Cited by Joshua M. Epstein, *The 1988 Defense Budget*, (Washington, D.C.: The Brookings Institution, 1987), p. 25.

19. CBO, *Reducing the Deficit: Spending and Revenue Options*, A Report to the Senate and House Committees on the Budget—Part II, March 1986, pp. 33–63.

20. Epstein, *The 1988 Defense Budget*, p. 31.

21. Ibid., p. 54.

CHAPTER 10

1. *Economic Report of the President 1988*, p. 300.

2. *Statistical Abstract of the United States 1988*, table 565, p. 342.

3. *Statistical Abstract of the United States 1987*, table 750. Even the data for persons, which include those living alone, are favorable. Among older persons, 12.6 percent were poor, compared to 14 percent for all persons. See ibid., table 747.

4. Ibid., tables 759, 760.

5. Henry J. Aaron, Harvey Galper, Joseph A. Pechman, George L. Perry, Alice M. Rivlin, and Charles L. Schultze, *Economic Choices 1987*, (Washington, D.C.: The Brookings Institution, 1986), p. 75.

6. *Statistical Abstract of the United States 1988*, table 588, p. 353; *Statistical Abstract of the United States 1979*, table 543, p. 345. Deflated by consumer price index.

7. Bureau of Labor Statistics.

8. *Statistical Abstract of the United States 1988*, table 471, p. 293, and table 670, p. 408.

9. Employment from ibid., table 1055, p. 608.

CHAPTER 11

1. *The Wall Street Journal*, August 24, 1988, p. 25.
2. Ibid., p. 14.
3. The following discussion is based on Congressional Budget Office (CBO), *An Analysis of the President's Budgetary Proposals for Fiscal Year 1989*, March 1988, pp. 33–57.
4. Office of the Assistant Secretary of Defense (Comptroller), *National Defense Estimates for FY 1988/1989*, April 1988, table 6.8, p. 88.
5. CBO, *An Analysis of the President's Budgetary Proposals for Fiscal Year 1989*, pp. 55–56.
6. Office of the Assistant Secretary of Defense (Comptroller), *National Defense Estimates for FY 1988/1989*, table 6.8, p. 88.
7. Ibid.

SELECTED
BIBLIOGRAPHY

Aaron, Henry J., Harvey Galper, Joseph A. Pechman, George L. Perry, Alice M. Rivlin, and Charles L. Schultze, *Economic Choices 1987* (Washington, D.C.: The Brookings Institution, 1986), p. 75.

Blinder, Alan S. *Hard Heads, Soft Hearts: Tough-Minded Economics for a Just Society* (Reading, MA: Addison-Wesley, 1987).

Boskin, Michael J. *Reagan and the Economy: The Successes, Failures and Unfinished Agenda* (San Francisco, CA: Institute for Contemporary Studies, 1987).

Congressional Budget Office. *An Analysis of the President's Budgetary Proposals for Fiscal Year 1989* (Washington, D.C.: GPO, March 1988).

————. *Reducing the Deficit: Spending and Revenue Options*, A Report to the Senate and House Committees on the Budget—Part II (Washington, D.C.: GPO, March 1986).

————. *Trident II Missiles: Capability, Costs, and Alternatives* (Washington, D.C.: GPO, 1986).

The Cuomo Commission on Trade and Competitiveness, *The Cuomo Commission Report: A New American Formula for a Strong Economy* (New York: Simon & Schuster, 1988).

Denison, Edward F. *Trends in American Economic Growth, 1929–1982* (Washington, D.C.: The Brookings Institution, 1985), p. 111.

Eisner, Robert. *How Real Is the Federal Deficit?* (New York: The Free Press, 1986).

Epstein, Joshua M. *The 1988 Defense Budget* (Washington, D.C.: The Brookings Institution, 1987).

Friedman, Benjamin. *Day of Reckoning: The Consequences of American Economic Policy Under Reagan and After* (New York: Random House, 1988).

Gordon, Robert J. *Macroeconomics.* 4th ed. (Boston, MA: Little,. Brown, 1987).

Harrison, Bennett, and Barry Bluestone. *The Great U-Turn: Corporate Restructuring and the Polarizing of America* (New York: Basic Books, 1988).

Kaufman, Richard F. "Causes of the Slowdown in Soviet Defense," *Soviet Economy* 1, 1 (1985): (1985) 9–12.

Kaufmann, William M. *A Reasonable Defense* (Washington, D.C.: The Brookings Institution, 1986), p. 14.

Malabre, Alfred L. Jr. *Understanding the Economy* (Homewood, IL: Dow Jones-Irwin, 1988).

Pechman, Joseph A. "Tax Reform: Theory and Practice," *Economic Perspectives* 1, 1 (Summer 1987): 19.

Peterson, Peter. *The Atlantic Monthly* (October 1987).

Phillips, A. W. H. "The Relation between Unemployment and the Rate of Change of Money Wage Rates in the United Kingdom, 1861–1957," *Economica* (November 1958): 283–99.

Reich, Robert. *The Next American Frontier* (New York: New York Times Books, 1983).

Rohatyn, Felix. "What Next?" *The New York Review of Books*, December 3, 1987: 3–5.

Schwartzman, David. *Games of Chicken: Four Decades of the American Nuclear Defense Policy* (New York: Praeger, 1988).

Stockman, David. *The Triumph of Politics* (New York: Avon, 1987).

Thurow, Lester C. *The Zero-Sum Solution: Building a World-Class American Economy* (New York: Simon & Schuster, 1985).

Weidenbaum, Murray. *Rendezvous with Reality: The American Economy After Reagan* (New York: Basic Books, 1988).

INDEX

ABOUT THE AUTHOR

A Canadian by birth, DAVID SCHWARTZMAN lives in New York City and is Professor of Economics in the Graduate Faculty of the New School for Social Research, where he has served as chairman of the Department of Economics. He previously taught at McGill, Columbia, and New York Universities. Between his early teaching stints, Schwartzman applied economics at the Dominion Bureau of Statistics in Canada. For several years he was a staff member of the National Bureau of Economic Research.

Schwartzman has served as a consultant to the Council of Wage and Price Stability, the Bureau of the Census, the Department of Justice, the Royal Commission on Farm Machinery of Canada, and in several antitrust cases.

Other books by the author are: *Decline of Service in Retail Trade, Oligopoly in the Farm Machinery Industry, Innovation in the Pharmaceutical Industry,* and *Games of Chicken: Four Decades of U.S. Nuclear Policy.*